BAKING MACARONS:
The Swiss Meringue Method

WRITTEN AND PHOTOGRAPHED BY
LISA MALIGA

Win free books, gift cards, and more! Subscribe to the Discerning Readers' Newsletter
http://eepurl.com/UZbE9

ISBN-978-0-692-15399-4

By the Author of
Baking Chocolate Cupcakes and Brownies: A Beginner's Guide
Baking French Macarons: A Beginner's Guide

Baking Macarons:
The Swiss Meringue Method

This unique cookbook is designed for bakers of all levels. Follow each carefully detailed recipe and bake stunning macarons that will impress any dessert lover.

Helpful information includes the best ingredients and equipment to stock your kitchen, resources, tips and troubleshooting, plus the easy macaronage technique that will save you time and energy.

With a photo of each recipe, Baking Macarons: The Swiss Meringue Method, offers everything you need to bake beautiful and delicious macarons. It features 20+ new tried-and-tested macaron recipes.

Some of the flavors include Minty Chocolate, Speculoos [Cookie Butter], Raspberry Cheesecake, and Apple Spice macarons.

TABLE OF CONTENTS

INTRODUCTION

Macarons are becoming increasingly popular to bake at home. At the grocery store, I noticed they carried three different brands of almond flour. A year ago, they only had one brand and it was in the health food aisle. The price of almond flour has also gone down, making these delicacies even more affordable.

I didn't plan to write a book about French macarons, let alone a second one about the Swiss meringue method. Then I joined a wonderful Facebook group, *All Things Macarons – Tips, Tricks and Techniques*. I'm so grateful for the generous and talented members who shared their expertise and encouraged macaron bakers of all levels. The Swiss method was discussed and shown, along with the [gasp!] use of a stand mixer to do the macaronage process. If you've made macarons, or even watched a video, you've seen how the baker uses a spatula to combine the wet [meringue] and dry [almond flour and confectioners' sugar] ingredients, which form the batter.

The macaronage process can be a bit tedious and time consuming. Some bakers recommend adding the dry ingredients to the meringue in three batches, others encourage you to dump it all in. Most opt for adding in two batches and carefully folding the mixture until it becomes glossy and is easy to pipe. The French method is the room temperature method but is very finicky and even if your macarons have the desired feet [*pied*], smooth tops, and nice dome like shapes, the insides may be hollow.

I've watched many videos on how to make macarons. I've read countless blogs where the author described his or her experiences with baking macarons. I've also bought and read numerous books where the author details the process of baking these small pastries. In only one book is the Swiss method written about and step-by-step photos shown. I include the book in my resources chapter.

Whether book, blog or video, the most common macaron baking instructions center around the French method, which is the use of "aged" egg whites. The other is the Italian method, which calls for heating up the sugar and water syrup to 118 degrees Celsius and then carefully pouring it in the meringue while it's being mixed. While some authors mention the fact that the Swiss method exists, many don't acknowledge it.

The few Swiss macaron videos I've seen are from European or South American bakers. One man did the entire process with a hand whisk. Others used a hand mixer, but none of them mixed all the ingredients in the mixer; the dry ingredients and meringue were done like that of the French and Italian methods.

It's amazing to see bakers of all skill levels using a variety of hand and stand mixers, but only for whipping the meringue. They don't use them as intended. Some are brand new, top of the line models with loads of power. These mixers are ready to work, but they are dismissed from their job function, replaced with a one-dollar rubber spatula.

The Swiss method I've discovered is innovative because it has two different features from the traditional one. 1. Granulated or caster sugar are not necessary. 2. After the meringue is ready, the almond flour/confectioners' sugar mixture is added to the bowl and mixed in a stand mixer for several seconds. You read that right, seconds, NOT minutes. No more macaronage by hand. This saves time, along with your shoulder and arm muscles. Best of all, it's quite effective when not overmixed.

As with *Baking French Macarons: A Beginner's Guide*, I go into a lot of detail about the technique needed to make these sweet little cookies. However, one thing hasn't changed between the time I first began baking macarons and now. I continued to experiment with the amounts and types of ingredients needed for baking perfect macaron shells. I had a unique and proven technique that I was ready to share with people who want to have macarons that look as good as they taste. I was proud of my petite cookies with the cute little feet, the shiny domelike shells and the crunchy thin skin of the cookie covering the chewy inner macaron. There were no hollows, only a spongy pair of cookies that held a luscious filling.

Baking Macarons: The Swiss Meringue Method covers the simple techniques you'll need along with the best type of equipment you should have to bake lovely macarons. You'll also learn how the weather makes a difference, why you should invest in a digital kitchen scale and oven thermometer. I've spent lots of time, money, and hard work to get these recipes right. They are all unique and some are more suited to those who like their macarons sweet and others who enjoy their macarons with a little less sugar and are more classically flavored.

These macarons only require three main ingredients, not the usual four. However, I add a couple of minor ones that will help stabilize the meringue and discourage those annoying hollows. This method is for any level of baker providing you carefully read each recipe thoroughly along with the helpful suggestions.

When you have the ingredients weighed and sifted, the egg whites separated, and the baking trays lined, it's time to bake macarons, Swiss style.

CHAPTER 1
RECOMMENDED EQUIPMENT

You may have some or all of the equipment and ingredients you need in your kitchen. If not, here's a list:

Heavy duty baking sheets/trays.

Before I first began baking macarons, I went to a discount store and bought two flimsy baking sheets. Then I had to buy more because they warped. I tried Wiltons brand and liked how sturdy they were but they were a little small for the silicone mats. Fortunately, I discovered Nordicware aluminum and they're just the right weight, are good quality, and reasonably priced. I have them in three different sizes and recommend them.

High quality baking sheets won't warp, or they certainly won't warp after a couple of uses. Dark baking sheets attract more heat than aluminum or stainless steel. The size most home bakers' use is called a half sheet. They're half the size of the sheets used by commercial bakers.

The size you get should be larger than the silicone mat, if that's what you'll use. My preferred size is 12.75" x 17.75" or above. The Silpats I use are sized at 11 5/8" x 16 1/2".

Once you find your preferred brand[s], stock up on them so you have enough if you make large amounts.

If you have budget type baking sheets, they might work but you'll have to double pan or stack them so they'll insulate the shells. Just make sure they're not warped.

Pastry bag/piping bag

There are three options, silicone, canvas, or disposable plastic. I've used canvas and it's nice and can be cleaned in a dishwasher or your washing machine. I haven't used silicone bags, but many amateur and professional bakers recommend them for their durability and compatibility with a variety of piping tips. Mostly, I use disposable plastic piping/decorating bags. Wilton is also easy to find, and crafts stores carry them along with their own brands. Online you can order several different brands and sizes.

For the record, a 12" bag is suitable for smaller macaron recipes, 14" for medium recipes, and 16" and above for larger recipes. Here's a guide.

Small =1egg white

Medium = 2 to 3 egg whites

Large = 4 or more egg whites.

Round piping tip[s]

I like the Ateco #802 round tip but you can use a larger one and/or a different brand like Wilton. The Wilton brand is found in crafts shops and discount stores so it's more readily available. For the filling, you can create some ganache or buttercream swirls by using a large star tip for a fancier filling. Or you can use a plain round tip. If using a piping bag, you can choose not to use a tip, especially with heavier ganaches and/or jam fillings.

Silicone mat[s]

Silicone mats

The Silpat brand comes in a variety of sizes and even includes one with 20 circles already printed on it. Many bakers only use the Silpat brand but there are several others that you can find online and in crafts or cookware stores. I've used the Velesco brand with similar results. Cleanup is very easy – soap and water followed by a lemon or vinegar rinse.

Parchment paper has its advantages and disadvantages. It's easy to find in most supermarkets and is reasonably priced. The problems I found are that it's hard to stay on the baking sheet. Some bakers use magnets, others glue it down with a dab of macaron batter. Even if the shells are removed cleanly, the paper will probably be wrinkled so it won't be reusable. Another advantage is the fact that it's one less item to wash.

Flexible silicone spatula

The key word here is flexible so it's easy to maneuver around the mixing bowl. When you get the right type of spatula, it will have the ability to scrape very easily. There are two reasons to choose silicone. 1. Flexibility and ease of use. 2. It won't scratch your mixing bowl. It's best to buy this in a store so you can test the grip and feel how comfortable it is in your hand. The handle will be made from silicone, plastic, wood or metal. I found a metal-handled silicone spatula at a discount store for less than $5 and it's quite sturdy. I recommend having at least two spatulas, as there should be one for fillings. A sturdy plastic spatula is fine for fillings, especially buttercreams. Even though you might use your mixer for the macaronage, you'll still need to scrape the sides and bottom of the bowl to make sure the wet and dry ingredients are fully incorporated.

Mesh sieve [strainer] [6" or 8"].

4 different sizes of sieves.

This tool is what will get your almond flour and confectioners' sugar ready for smooth macarons. These are easy to find in most grocery and discount stores. I've seen them for as low as $3. Try getting a stainless steel one with one or two little prongs that attach to your bowl.

Another type of sieve is actually a flour sifter. Some people are more comfortable using this type of sifter as they grew up in a household where it was used or they just naturally prefer it. Many models have rotary crank handles, while others have a handle you can squeeze in order to sift the dry ingredients. You can purchase these sifters online and in kitchen supply stores.

I've used fine mesh strainers for making fine sugar out of granulated sugar. I've also run confectioners' sugar through them. They're nice for those of you who either don't have a food processor or have plenty of time and patience. Even if you purchase finely ground almond flour, it will take a long time to push the grains through a fine sifter.

Stainless steel or glass mixing bowls

When mixing egg whites and sugar to form a meringue, the best choice is a stainless steel bowl. The inside of the bowl is strong, smooth, and easy to clean. Stainless steel resists trapping fats or proteins like plastic does. Glass is the second best choice for making meringue. The reason it's not as good as stainless steel is due to the slippery surface. It also can be heavier to lift. When making chocolate ganaches, glass is an excellent choice as a double boiler [*bain-marie*].

Copper bowl

For the purist who wants to make a meringue, copper is the best choice. Most won't work with a stand mixer but will with a hand mixer. For more information about the science behind whipping egg whites in a copper bowl, check out this article from *Popular Science* magazine.

https://www.popsci.com/beat-egg-whites-in-copper-bowl#page-4

Plastic mixing bowls

When making fillings for your macarons, a large plastic bowl serves the purpose. Easy to find, inexpensive, and great for the job. Have more than one on hand. Plastic is more porous than stainless steel or glass so that's why it's fine for what goes inside the macarons, just not the macaron shells.

Stand or hand mixer

Hand mixers.

For the first three dozen batches, I only used a hand mixer. It was several years old and came with standard beaters and a handy whisk attachment. Then I bought a stand mixer, the mini, which is the smallest size Kitchen Aid makes. The bowl only holds three and a half quarts and it's perfect for small to medium sized batches of macarons. The whisk attachment is included, along with a flat beater, but I bought the flex edge beater, which is ideal for the macaronage process. The stand mixer is usually more powerful than a hand mixer, and it allows you to do other things when whipping the meringue. For the macaronage process, it's so much easier and quicker to use a mixer than doing it by hand.

Saucepan

For the Swiss method, you'll need a saucepan that is slightly smaller than your mixing bowl. It should be fairly deep so that the water doesn't touch the bottom of the bowl.

Food processer [optional]

A food processor will finely grind your almonds. You'll still need to sieve your almond flour and confectioners' sugar, but you'll only have to do it once.

Balloon whisk

I've discovered this is the best way to mix the egg whites and sugar together when heating up the Swiss meringue.

Measuring spoons/cups

If you do any baking, you should have these. Stainless steel is recommended for the spoons and cups, or glass for the cups.

Cooling rack/s

You should have at least one to help your cookies cool off.

Oven thermometer

This is the only way to make sure your oven is the correct temperature. The digital display on my oven may read 300 but when the thermometer indicates it's 280 degrees. I trust that number. For baking macarons, you will need one of these to make sure the temperature is accurate. I've had to learn how to set my oven so that it'll stay in the vicinity of 300 degrees. Oven thermometers can be found at most grocery/discount stores for about five dollars. This cost is definitely worth it.

Candy thermometer [optional]

While not necessary, if you have one, use it to get the egg whites and sugar mixture up to around 130 F.

Toothpicks

Handy to have for popping any extra air bubbles you might find after tapping your freshly piped macaron shells.

Digital scale

Digital scale that measures in grams and ounces. An oven thermometer is important for making sure the temperature is accurate. These two tools will help you achieve macaron baking success!

To accurately weigh your ingredients, a digital scale is a must-have. Most macaron recipes are in grams and the precision can help your macarons succeed. You can find them at many discount stores, kitchen/bakery supply stores, and online.

Covered storage containers/storage bags

I have these in a variety of sizes and they vary in use for mixing the almond/sugar mixtures to storing the finished macarons. When they go into the freezer, I always double wrap the macarons in a sturdy storage bag.

Wax paper

Never use wax paper to bake your macarons! However, wax paper is very handy to line a plate or tray so you can rest and later fill your macarons.

Paper macaron template

Highly recommended. You can download them online or even buy a silicone mat with the circles [or other shapes] already printed on them. Remember to remove the template when you're done piping your macarons.

CHAPTER 2
MACARON SHELL INGREDIENTS

Ingredients for the macaron shells and filling

Another advantage to baking your own macarons is that you have control over the quality of your ingredients. You can choose organically grown ingredients, eggs from hens that are ethically treated, organic almond flour, or opt for pistachio flour or another nut/gluten-free type of flour. Love cookie butter macarons but can't find them online? Now you can make your own. And yes, I have included a recipe for cookie butter macarons.

Here is a list of ingredients to make your wonderful macarons.

Macaron Shell Ingredients

- **Finely ground** almond flour. First of all, almond flour and almond meal is the same thing. If you have access to buying almonds in bulk, stock up. Blanched almonds are recommended if you're looking for a very smooth shell, and they'll have to be **very finely ground** up in a food processor. Notice how I'm stressing that it needs to be finely ground. I've used Bob's Red

Mill, King Arthur brands and more recently the Mandelin brand. Trader Joe's also sells it, but it's from unskinned almonds, not blanched. Of course, there are many available brands. The price is around $8-12 per pound, which explains why macarons cost up to $3.00 each. Even if you get finely ground almond flour, you still have to sift it at least one to three more times! Unsifted or minimally sifted almond flour will make your macarons look lumpy. Since I began making macarons in early 2016, I've noticed the price of almond flour has dropped and more brands are available. While almond flour is the most commonly used nut flour, just about any finely ground nut flour can be used. Hazelnut, walnut, and pistachio nut flours are the most common.

One word of warning—there is a Spanish brand sold in the UK that de-oils their almond flour for an extra fine texture. You want fine almond flour but it should retain the natural oil. So make sure that your almond flour is finely ground, but not de-oiled.

- Confectioners' sugar [powdered sugar or icing sugar]. In America, most brands are labeled 10X and contain 3% cornstarch. If allergic to corn, you can find this type of sugar mixed with a small amount of tapioca starch. The 10X does NOT mean it's been sifted ten times, it's the size of the mesh screens that are used to separate powered sugar into three different sizes: 4X, 10X and14X. 14X is considered the finest, but 10X is the most commonly found in stores.

- Egg whites. Unlike the French method, they don't have to be aged. What's aging egg whites? Aged means that they've been out of the shell for several hours, days or even a week [or two]. I haven't noticed much difference although there are macaron bakers who are convinced that the longer an egg white ages, the more moisture has evaporated. It's also supposed to increase the elasticity of the whites, thus helping to prevent runniness, which might ruin your macarons. With the Swiss method, you can use fresh eggs at any temperature other than frozen. As for egg whites from a carton, they are pasteurized so bear that in mind. Some bakers prefer using them and have excellent results; others have trouble making the meringue. As for egg quality, I prefer using eggs that come from chickens not cooped up in tiny cages. While 'free roaming' eggs cost more, they taste better.

- Arrowroot powder/flour. This ingredient may help conquer those hollows. I began using arrowroot several years ago when I was making foot and body powders. The silky smooth texture is so nice on the skin. It comes from the root of a tropical plant *Maranta arundinacea* and has been used in sauces as a thickener. It works nicely in macaron shells. The one thing it can't do is thicken a buttercream or any filling containing dairy products.

- Cornstarch [or corn flour] can be used instead of arrowroot. Make sure the label reads gluten-free. It's less expensive and easier to find than arrowroot. It's also ideal for thickening dairy products like buttercream filling.

- Cream of tartar. You should be able to find this in your grocery store. I've noticed it goes on sale around the fall baking season. It's used to help the meringue achieve stability.

- Powdered egg whites. For those of you who live in a hot or humid climate, the addition of powdered egg whites will help stabilize the eggs, and may help prevent hollow shells. Sometimes labeled as egg protein powder, check the label to make sure it only contains powdered egg whites and no other ingredient[s], Use as a substitute for arrowroot powder.

- Colorant[s]. I've used three types of colorants: powdered, powdered made with natural ingredients, and gel colorants. Gel colorants are also excellent for brightening the color of your buttercream filling. Wilton gel colorants are available in your crafts store or discount store and online. The icing color is often used and it's added with a knife or toothpick. For the past year, I've used AmeriColor or Chefmaster as they are packaged in a squeeze bottle. Gel colors require only a few drops to achieve beautiful colors.

- Extracts/flavor emulsions/essential oils. I currently don't use any of these as I like to keep the shells as is and let the filling contribute all the flavor. What is the difference between them? Extracts consist of alcohol and the intended flavor. For example, lemon extract contains 90% alcohol, oil of lemon and a tiny bit of water. Remember, alcohol burns off during baking so you won't get that flavor but the aroma and taste of the lemon remain strong.

In addition, not all extracts are created equal. For example, the almond extract for a major brand contains water, alcohol, and oil of bitter almond. In a brand designed for more serious cooks, the ingredients are alcohol, oil of bitter almond, and water. As you can see, one brand waters theirs down, the other one doesn't. The difference will be tasted in the finished dessert.

While I haven't personally used flavor emulsions, they are thick liquids that won't change the consistency of your macaron batter. Oftentimes, they contain flavor and coloring, for example, LorAnn's Red Velvet is obviously red and has a chocolaty/citrusy aroma and taste from what I've read.

Essential oils can be used in the shells but only a few drops are needed. The essential oil must be pure, therapeutic grade and contain NO other additives, like olive or grapeseed oil, to be effective.

Macaron Filling Ingredients

I've been experimenting with making more creative fillings. Let's face it, the filling is what flavors the macarons. While some of the buttercreams contain a cup or two of confectioners' sugar, in some recipes I was able to decrease the amount significantly. For the American buttercream filling, keep in mind that the better the butter, the better the filling!

- High quality butter [President, Kerrygold, Plugra or any fresh high fat non-GMO local butter]. Unsalted butter is recommended. Also, the butter should be at room temperature when you're making the filling.

- High quality vanilla extract, vanilla beans, vanilla bean powder OR vanilla bean paste. Yes, it costs more but the flavor is worth it. Imitation vanilla extract is very inexpensive but it isn't nearly as good. I recommend real vanilla beans, powder or paste as it's flavorful and contains the tiny seeds. These types of vanilla are ideal for flavoring macaron shells.

- For a rich, flavorful buttercream, use organic heavy cream. High fat creams always taste better! You won't need to use a lot.

- Cream cheese. When baking cupcakes I finally got around to using a cream cheese frosting. Not quite as sweet as butter, it's perfect for sugary macarons. And what better ingredient for a cheesecake flavored macaron?

- Mascarpone Cheese. This is a rich creamy additive to your macaron fillings. Mascarpone cheese is similar to ricotta except for the fact that it's made from cream and not milk. I'd never used it before. However, I was pleased with how easily it blended with butter when I put it in the mixer. My first recipe using this lovely Italian cheese also combines honey and fig jam.

- Jam filling. Use either a natural jam/fruit spread or fresh fruit. Making a filling with fresh fruit is a little more work, but the taste is a lot better.

- Extracts/flavor emulsions/essential oils. I used a coconut extract for my buttercream and it was a very good flavor. Not excellent, but I'd make it again as it seemed to be a nice interpretation of coconut.

I prefer using essential oils as I already have several for my soapmaking. I'm very comfortable working with essential oils. Peppermint is awesome when added to chocolate. Many other essential oils can be used to enhance chocolate and/or buttercreams: lime and just about any citrus essential oil. You can use lavender, rose, allspice [pimento], ginger, spearmint, cornmint, sage or even cinnamon bark -- but go easy! Pure essential oils are very potent, so you'll only need a drop or two for your batch. Always start with just one drop and taste before adding more. Make sure you buy a genuine food-grade essential oil that is NOT diluted with grapeseed or olive oil.

CHAPTER 3
TIPS & TROUBLESHOOTING

One of your goals may be to have
hollow-free macarons as seen here.

Our dainty diva cookies are more difficult to make than oatmeal raisin or chocolate chip cookies. Although they contain only three or four ingredients, these little cookies are all about technique. Macarons require your undivided attention. When making them, you're concentrating only on this finicky dessert. Don't make them when you're cooking another meal, running the dishwasher, or washing dishes by hand.

Tips

- Triple sift/sieve almond flour and store in an airtight container. Label and date it if storing for more than a week.

- Each time you sift your almond flour, you'll have small pieces left. Save them and use them to put in your breakfast cereal or oatmeal. Alternatively, you can use them as a skin exfoliator, so save it in a small container until you have enough.

- Make or find a template online so you have a piping guide [unnecessary if using *marked* silicone mats]. I've included a free template link in CHAPTER 12: Recommended Books & Websites.

- It's easier to separate cold eggs. However, for the Swiss method, it doesn't matter if the egg whites are straight from the refrigerator or room temperature. Make sure there aren't bits of yolk or eggshells in the whites. Even a tiny amount of yolk will damage the batter, so if you're breaking them and a bit of yolk falls into the whites, you'll need to start over. Need help with how to effectively, and quickly, separate eggs? Here are four ways to do it: http://www.wikihow.com/Separate-an-Egg

- For your meringue, I recommend a stainless steel or glass mixing bowl. Copper is the best, but can be quite costly!

- Once your meringue is ready, add the flour/sugar mixture right away. Meringue isn't something that you can let sit around as it deflates quickly.

- Your utensils and bowls must be CLEAN! Wash and dry them thoroughly before using. Any water or dirt in your mixing bowl or on any utensil/s might cause your macaron shells to crack or not develop feet. I recommend using white vinegar, fresh lemons, or baking soda.

- Use a tall plastic cup or glass to hold your piping bag. For the macaron filling, add your round tip to the bag, twist the bag to avoid any leakage, and place inside the cup so the tip is facing up. Put the ends of the bag over the glass so it forms a cuff. [I have links at the back of the book for recommended tip sizes.]

- Cookie sheets should be doubled to prevent your delicate macaron shells from browning.

- After piping your macarons, always bang the cookie sheets on the counter several times. You can fold a towel and place it on the counter to help make this part a little quieter.

- Let the macarons dry for at least 30 minutes. If possible, set up a floor or table fan nearby to help speed up the drying process. You'll know they're done when you touch the side of one and none of the batter sticks to your finger.

- Use a reliable digital scale that measures in ounces and grams. They cost as little as $10. If you plan to make many batches of macarons, this is a worthwhile investment.

- The paddle attachment on your stand mixer is ideal for the mixer macaronage.

- A silicone spatula is recommended. You'll need one that is thin and flexible. The head should be plain and not have a hook on one side.

- Make sure you scrape the sides and bottom of your mixing bowl when doing the macaronage process so that flour, sugar and egg whites are completely combined.

- When making buttercream filling, SIFT in your powdered sugar so it yields a smoother filling. Oftentimes, powdered sugar contains lumps due to age and/or humidity.

- Jam and jelly fillings will seep through macaron shells faster than buttercream or heavier fillings like peanut butter and chocolate ganache. Therefore, make a smaller batch or be prepared to eat your macarons quickly!

- Ideally, macaron shells will be easy to remove from the silicone mat or parchment paper. However, if they stick, please don't get frustrated and try to wrestle them off the surface. In some cases, returning them to the oven for a minute or two may help. Then again, it may not. Use a sharp knife, cheese slicer, or small spatula to pry them off. I've not had any luck in the steaming method of pouring hot water beneath the baking sheet, but you might. Sometimes I throw them away, especially if they come off in bits and chunks. The birds enjoy eating them. However, all isn't lost when that happens. You can crumble them up and sprinkle them on top of your favorite ice cream.

- Don't fill your macaron shells until they've cooled off, as you don't want your filling to melt. Also, make sure you let your macaron shells cool off for at least 10 minutes before removing them from the parchment paper or silicone mat.

- Most cookies taste great as soon as they come out of the oven. Macarons don't, as they're a bit hard and crispy. Not only should they be served at room temperature, they should also be served about 24 hours later. Have one that's just been filled, but I guarantee you that if you wait, you'll love them even more. The flavors will meld together and the shell will still have that nice crunchy texture on the outside, and the chewy texture on the inside.

- If you've never made macarons before, it's not advisable to make them when it's super hot, the humidity's high and/or it's raining. Macarons dislike moisture. Unless you have a kitchen with double pane glass windows, a northern exposure, and everything's well sealed, I don't recommend trying it.

- For those of you who live in a humid area, if you bake lots of macarons and/or plan on selling them, invest in a dehumidifier. It will make a difference.

- Adding powdered egg whites will help stabilize the eggs when it's hot or humid in your area. Use as a substitute for arrowroot powder.

- If you don't use all your filling, you can place your piping bag inside a heavy duty Ziploc bag and freeze it for up to 3 months. Make sure you label and date it.

- Take notes when you're making your macarons. I print out each recipe and make notes on the back of it. I calculate the time I start, how long each process takes, how many shells I pipe, how many turn out correctly, how many don't, and how many minutes each batch bakes. I do periodic oven spot checks and note the temperature. Please see CHAPTER 10: The Recipe Guide.

- If you don't take notes, photograph or videotape your macaron baking, so you can see the process afterwards. I find it very helpful to record the egg whites/sugar mixing, whipping the meringue, and mixer macaronage parts so I can see how long each element takes.

- Note the time when you finished piping your first batch of macarons. That way you can tell how long they rest until they are dry enough to put in the oven.

- If possible, keep pets and young children away from the baking area.

- Cleaning silicone mats is simple if you use very hot water and baking soda and fresh lemon or vinegar.

- Bake only one tray of macarons at a time. This isn't time or energy-efficient, but it helps bake the macarons evenly and you can determine if there are any trouble areas this way.

- Meringue can't be refrigerated or frozen, it must be piped and baked just after it's been made.

Troubleshooting

Cracked shells are usually caused by three things.

1. Not tapping your trays just after piping your macaron shells.
2. Using a single cookie sheet. I tried on two occasions to use one cookie sheet on the center oven rack. Many of the shells exploded like miniature volcanoes. I managed to save a few as I added another cookie sheet, which worked very well to insulate the shells.

3. Not resting your macaron shells long enough. The shells should go from wet to having a matte finish. Depending upon the temperature and humidity in your area, macaron shells generally dry within 30-45 minutes. If you're in a desert or low humidity area, you can have fully dry shells within a few minutes. If you live in a high humidity area, it may take as long as 2 hours for your shells to acquire the matte finish.

Browned macaron shells

Using one cookie sheet, especially one that is lightweight, isn't recommended due to the fact that you'll either burn your shells or they'll come out far browner than what you'd like.

Some gel colorants can cause your shells to brown faster than normal.

Splotchy macaron shells

Too much oil in the almond flour. Sometimes this happens when you don't shake the container of gel paste colorant. If it is oily almond flour, you can fix the problem by spreading the flour on a parchment or Silpat covered baking sheet and dry in the oven for about ten minutes at a low temperature like 200-210 degrees Fahrenheit/95-100 degrees Celsius.

Macaron shells have no feet

Usually this is the result of undermixed batter.

Macaron shells are wrinkled

The good thing about them is that they usually aren't hollow. However, they don't look as good as a perfectly smooth top. The culprit is usually a low oven temperature. Mine happened when the oven reached 260 degrees Fahrenheit. The problem was solved when I increased the oven temperature.

When making chocolate macarons, adding too much cocoa powder can cause your shells to wrinkle.

Another culprit can be oily almond flour. Drying the almond flour in the oven on a very low heat setting, 200-210 degrees Fahrenheit/95-100 degrees Celsius for about ten minutes may help.

Macaron shells are lopsided.

This can be an oven issue – the times it happened to me, the oven was running too hot.

Lumpy macarons

Rustic looking macarons are the result of not sifting your flour and sugar enough. For best results, sift the almond flour three times, removing any bits that don't pass though the sieve. Sift the confectioners' sugar once. Then sift both the flour and sugar together once.

If using a food processor, mix the two ingredients together so the almond flour doesn't turn into almond paste. You'll still need to sift the almond flour and sugar together at least once.

Misshapen macaron shells

Hollow macaron shells

This is the result of not piping your macaron batter correctly. Piping round and same-sized macaron shells takes practice. You'll get better at piping with every batch you make. Also, make sure you use a template.

Macarons are hollow

This is a very common problem even when someone has made several batches. You can have a gorgeous domed shiny shell, lovely ruffled feet – and a gaping black hole where there should be a spongy interior.

There are two types of hollow, the half hollow, which has some sponginess to the insides, and the full hollow, which is a thin shell hiding an air pocket.

Usually the culprit is the meringue. Undermixing will cause hollows. This is why paying close attention to how long the meringue takes is recommended. For me, meringue takes 8-9 minutes to reach the firm peak. Any less, hollows. Any more, hollows. The reason I'm stressing the amount of time is that I paid close attention to the starting time and the stopping time. For you, it may be a little longer or a little shorter, because it depends on the size of your mixer and the speed that you set it on. I have a small stand mixer, the KitchenAid Artisan Mini, which has a 3.5-quart bowl. If you have another brand, or a KitchenAid Professional, it may take less time. Also, some bakers recommend mixing at high speed right away, others suggest starting it at a low speed and gradually increasing it. I'm in the latter school, as I baby the meringue.

As egg whites don't have to age like in the French method, that's not an issue here. Another culprit is the macaronage mixing whether it's with the stand mixer or by hand. Over-mixing usually results in no hollow but with a flat surface and sometimes they're without feet. Slightly under-mixing may result in half hollows.

As many bakers know, heat and humidity can affect your macarons. Using powdered egg whites will strengthen your meringue and may help reduce hollows.

Hollows are also caused in the oven when the macarons are underbaked. This is why I recommend trying to peel off one of the shells. If it clings to the mat or paper, it's not done. Try testing it again in another minute or two. If an underbaked macaron is hollow, it's because the interior collapsed. Drying upside down may help with the hollows.

The oven temperature may also be causing your macarons to inflate/deflate too quickly. While 300 Fahrenheit [150 Celsius] is usually the ideal temperature, it may not be for your macarons. Try increasing or decreasing the temperature by a few degrees and see what happens. Make sure you write down what the ideal temperature is.

If your oven only has a top heating element, use the one level below the center rack. An oven stone [or a large cookie sheet on the bottom shelf] may help distribute the heat better, thus eliminating hollows.

Hollows don't bother everyone whether it's a family member or friend who samples your macarons. Some bakers don't really care, just as long as they look good and have feet. When I first began baking macarons, I was more interested in getting round, domed and footed macarons. Then the hollow problem bothered me, as I'm a perfectionist. I read as much as I could about the problems and solutions.

Know Your Oven!

Ever since I began baking macarons, I've had problems with my oven. This is why I always use an oven thermometer. My oven may read 300 degrees Fahrenheit but when I look at the oven thermometer, I see that it's 320. Then it'll read 310 a few minutes later. I used to have an oven that was too cold – I'd set it at 320 and the temperature wouldn't budge past 300.

So, no matter if you have a gas, electric, convection or toaster oven, always, always get an oven thermometer and test your temperature. Where are the hot spots? Once you bake a batch of macarons, note if any are browner or darker. Then see where that corresponds to in your oven. Know about the all-important heating element – is it on the top, the bottom or located on the top and bottom. Calibrate it if you can. Consult your owner's manual or Google the brand name and model number and learn more about adjusting the temperature.

Here are some handy tips:

- Test your oven temperature with an oven thermometer. Most home ovens aren't calibrated, so that's why a thermometer is a must-have when baking macarons. General oven temperatures vary but many macaron shells are baked at the 300-degree range [150 Celsius]. Also, make sure your oven's at the right temperature when the preheat beeper sounds. Mine used to be at 180 degrees Fahrenheit when that happened!

- If you have an electric oven or an older oven, you'll probably notice more hot spots and uneven temperatures. Don't be discouraged, just monitor your oven temperature and your batches and you'll get great looking macarons.

- Note where your heating element is: above or below. If you have problems with macarons being too brown, put an empty cookie sheet on the oven rack directly above the macarons if the heating element is on top. Conversely, if it's below, put the empty baking sheet below them.

- If your macarons are underbaked or not baking correctly when they're on the center rack, you should move them up or down one level, depending on the location of your heating element.

- Ovens vary. Some have hot spots, which mean you should be aware of them so you can set your cookie sheets accordingly. Some are very well heated throughout. The instructions for convection ovens vary slightly and you can't put your trays directly in front of the fan.

- If you've located hot spots in your oven, you can pipe your macaron shells in a different pattern so that they'll all bake evenly.

- If your oven is running hot during the baking process, open the door for a few minutes to lower the temperature. Alternatively, you can slat the door open with the handle of a wooden spoon.

- If your oven is maintaining its temperature, the only time you want to open the door is to rotate the tray midway through the baking process.

- If your oven is underheating, then you don't want to open the door to let any of the hot air out. This is when you should increase your oven temperature by a few degrees.

- Let your oven preheat for a minimum of 30 minutes.

- NOTE: You can use a toaster oven as long as it's 1500 watts.

CHAPTER 4
COLORING MACARON SHELLS

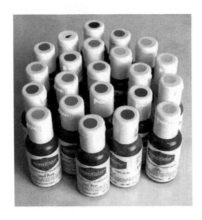

Gel food colorants

One way to make your macarons look enticing is to color them. The color can also be representative of the flavor. For example, blueberry will be blue, lemon will be yellow, green tea will be, you guessed it, green, etc. As macaron shells are so sensitive to liquids being added, standard food coloring isn't recommended as it contains water. Yes, some bakers add several drops of the type of food coloring and they turn out fine. However, I never felt comfortable risking a batch by adding liquid coloring. Although I tried to avoid that mistake, I still made it with adding too much gel colorant and got green and brown shells rather than the lime green color I was seeking. I didn't think it was possible, but the browned shells were the biggest clue that I'd been trying too hard to get green shells.

Since I also craft soap, I had lots of mica colorants in my soap closet. However, the shimmery purple mica colorant designed for soap didn't work in macaron shells – certainly nothing shimmered and the color turned out more gray than purple.

I've discovered that some powdered additives/natural colorants like cocoa powder and Matcha green tea powder, make the batter a bit heavier and harder to mix. The first time I made chocolate macarons I added more cocoa powder than necessary in order to get the desired brown color. This was back when I was doing the French meringue method, and I worked up quite a sweat hand mixing it into the meringue. Even if these natural additives are sifted, they'll still affect the macaronage process so be careful not to add too much.

If using powdered color, add to the almond/sugar mixture rather than the meringue. However, if using a gel colorant, it's best to add that to the meringue. Powder mixes better with dry ingredients, gel mixes better with wet ones.

Powdered colorants can be added to the meringue just before reaching firm peak, or to the dry ingredients. I've tried both methods and they work equally well. Several companies in America and other countries make powdered food colorants. Two of the larger ones are Lorann and AmeriColor. I've tested some of the Lorann powdered colors and find they color the shells very well.

Since I love bright colored macarons, I'm now using gel colors, the majority of them are from the AmeriColor company, but have tried some from Chefmaster. Both companies offer their selection of colorants in a convenient squeeze bottle. They are easy to add to the meringue. Only a few drops are needed, so a small bottle will last for quite a while.

Whatever brand or type of colorant you choose, always check that brand's recommended measurements as some colorants require a tiny amount while others require more. It's recommended that you start with a tiny amount and add more, if necessary. With any gel-based colorant, I recommend shaking the container before using.

The shells and fillings in this book are the results of gel-based colors. When going for bold colors, you can see how vivid the colors are. Your results will differ if you use a different brand or type of colorant, or if you prefer a darker or lighter shade.

CHAPTER 5
PIPING BAGS & TIPS

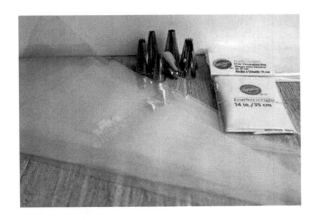

Even if you've never held a piping/pastry/icing bag before, you can still pipe nice round and similar-sized macaron shells.

Use a round tip. The best size for the Wilton brand ranges from 7 to 12. I prefer the #10 size. With Ateco, I use the #802. Smaller tips help get rid of air bubbles. You may have better luck with a smaller or larger size. Practice and then when you find that right size, make sure you have an extra one as a backup. Ateco is another brand and they can be ordered online or purchased at such stores as Williams-Sonoma, Sur la Table or Bed, Bath & Beyond.

You can use just a piping bag and cut the edge off the bottom and don't use a tip at all. This can work, but I recommend it more for piping heavier fillings like ganache.

Maybe you plan to make macarons just once. If so, don't invest in piping bags and/or tips; just use a gallon size Ziploc bag. All you do is cut a quarter-inch size on a bottom corner and there's your homemade piping bag.

Most plastic disposable piping bags range from 12", 14" or 16" and more in length. Bags are usually sold in packs of 10, 12 or 100. For your convenience, I'm repeating the bag size you'll need as it correlates to the number of egg whites for your macaron batter.

12" bag is suitable for smaller macaron recipes, 14" for medium recipes and 16" and above for larger recipes.

Small =1egg white

Medium = 2 – 3 egg whites

Large = 4 or more egg whites.

For frostings and fillings, it's better to have a larger bag like a 14" or a 16" so that you don't run out of room. I remember cramming as much buttercream filling into a small piping bag as possible and having it escape from the top of the bag and fall to the counter.

The easiest way to fill your piping bag is to add the tip and then cut off the bottom part of the bag. Generally, this will be about 1/4" or so. Place it in a tall cup or glass to fill. You don't want the batter pouring out of the pastry bag just yet. Twist near the bottom to prevent any mixture from escaping, then place into the cup with the tip facing upwards. The bag should be taller than the cup. You can form a cuff over the rim so it's simple to add the batter.

After you pour and/or spoon in the batter, it's time to release any excess air and close the top with a rubberband or a piping bag tie.

> Filling a piping bag
> **https://youtu.be/-X7i1QKAvuA**

> Piping macarons demonstration by pastry chef Mario Zumbo. He's demonstrating this technique without using a tip. Some people prefer this time-saving method.
> **https://youtu.be/_MAeJqFGr3s**

The piping part gets easier with every batch. I still have to remember to squeeze from the top and let gravity help me out!

Here are some more tips for piping nice, round macaron shells.

- Scrape the batter into the piping bag. After it's filled, lay the bag lengthwise on top of a paper towel and push the batter down so there aren't any air pockets. Do this gently but firmly, using a ruler or a plastic dough scraper. Then twist the top. You might want to put a rubber band on it so the batter doesn't ooze out the top.

- Hold with your dominant hand and with your other hand direct the tip vertically. Count to three as you're piping each macaron cookie. Then lift up quickly and do the next. You don't want little peaks to form on the top because that usually means your batter's undermixed. However, if the batter is just right, the peak will flatten, especially after you tap the tray on the counter.

- If you're right handed, start piping the shells on the left side of the mat, reverse if you're left handed.

- Piping is much easier when you use a template. These are free and easy to find online and download, I've provided a link for them in CHAPTER 12: Recommended Books & Websites. Also, you can purchase macaron mats with the circles already printed on them.

- Tip-saving Tip! For chocolate ganache recipes, the best type of tip is usually no tip at all. I learned this the hard way when making a chocolate ganache with acai powder that thickened overnight. I also tried adding bits of chopped up bar chocolate to a peppermint buttercream frosting and having larger bits get stopped at the top part of the tip. If you don't use a tip, you can cut a larger hole in your disposable piping bag.

CHAPTER 6
MEASUREMENT EQUIVALENTS

Liquid/dry measurements

U.S.	Everywhere Else
1/4 teaspoon	1.25 ml
1/2 teaspoon	2.5 ml
1 teaspoon	5 ml
1 Tablespoon	15 ml
1/8 Cup or 1 ounce	30 ml
1/4 Cup or 2 ounces	60 ml
1/3 Cup or 2 2/3 ounces	80 ml
1/2 Cup or 4 ounces	120 ml
3/4 Cup or 6 ounces	177 ml
1 Cup or 8 ounces	240 ml
2 Cups [1 pint] or 16 ounces	480 ml
4 Cups [1 quart] or 32 ounces	960 ml

Oven Temperatures

Fahrenheit	Celsius
250 degrees	120 degrees
275 degrees	140 degrees
300 degrees	150 degrees
325 degrees	165 degrees
350 degrees	180 degrees
375 degrees	190 degrees

CHAPTER 7
BAKING CHECKLIST

- Note outside and inside temperature and humidity just before you begin baking.

- Have a notepad and pen handy so you can take notes.

- In addition to taking notes, photograph/film the process. Or have someone photograph/film you so you can concentrate on baking.

- Is your almond flour sifted [at least 3 times] or ground in the food processor?

- Have you premixed your almond flour and confectioners' sugar? Have they been sifted together once?

- Are your egg whites weighed?

- Is your confectioners' [icing] sugar sifted and measured?

- Are your mixing bowls clean and dry?

- Are your parchment paper or silicone mats clean, dry and ready for piping?

- Have you added a tip to the piping bag?

- Are the oven racks in the correct position?

- Will you make your filling after your macaron shells or is it already made?

- Is your cooling rack set out?

- Are your drying/filling trays lined with wax paper?

Use this as a guide to help monitor the baking process:

- First batch: # shells sat for # minutes. Baked for # minutes.

- Second batch: # shells baked for # minutes.

- Third batch: # shells baked for # minutes.

- With each batch, note the type of cookie sheet, whether you use only one or if you double them. Also, note the position of the oven rack.

- Indicate if you're using parchment paper or silicone mats.

- Observe the temperature of your oven periodically.

- Note when you rotated the baking sheet.

CHAPTER 8
THE STAGES IN PHOTOS

Meringue ingredients for macarons

Meringue ingredients, clockwise from top: almond flour/confectioners' sugar blend, confectioners' sugar, cream of tartar, arrowroot powder, and egg whites.

4 Basic Stages in Pictures

1 - Cooked Sugar

The Swiss method consists of cooking your sugar and egg whites to about 125-130 degrees Fahrenheit. This takes only 1 to 2 minutes.

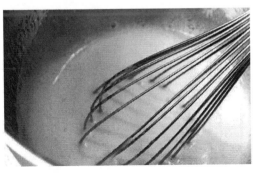

2 - Firm Peak [bird's beak] bec d'oiseau

Firm peak, or what the French refer to as bird's beak, *bec d'oiseau*, is when the egg whites are soft enough to gently curve downwards. This may take about 6-10 minutes if using a stand mixer set on medium-high or high speed. When you remove the whisk attachment, notice how the egg whites form the shape of a bird's beak. Also, note how smooth and glossy the meringue is.

In my other macaron book, I mentioned that the meringue should be at stiff peak stage, although I called it the North Star because it's pointing in that direction when you flip the whisk attachment upside down. With the Swiss meringue method, due to the heating up of the sugar and egg whites to achieve more stability, it only needs to be at firm peak.

3 - Mixer macaronage.

Add ALL of your almond/ confectioners' sugar blend into the mixing bowl and let your stand mixer do what it's supposed to do – mix it up for you. Use low to medium speeds and watch the process very carefully. This will only take a few seconds, not minutes! WARNING: DON'T rush the process by turning your mixer to high speed or you will over mix.

While using a paddle attachment is recommended, you can save time by using the whisk attachment.

4 - Ribbons

The ribbons you'll be looking for are those in the macaronage process that indicate the meringue and the almond flour/sugar blend is ready to be poured into the piping bag. Even if you use the mixer macaronage method, you should always scrape the sides and especially the bottom of the bowl to make certain the wet and dry ingredients are fully incorporated. The batter should be shiny. Test it by lifting the spatula above the mixing bowl and watch how the mixture flows in such a way as to create ribbons of batter. You can also check to make sure it's ready by lifting the spatula and writing the number 8 with the batter.

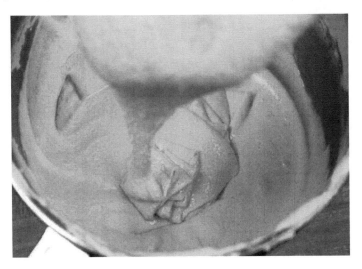

CHAPTER 9
MACARON SHELL RECIPES

Basic Macaron Shells

All the recipes in this book contain confectioners' sugar [icing sugar] rather than superfine or caster sugar. What looks like a lot of confectioners' sugar is actually a similar amount of granulated sugar. However, the particles in confectioners' sugar are so fine that more is needed. Another benefit is that confectioners' sugar produces smoother looking shells.

The confectioners' sugar should be mixed with the egg whites before being heated, so there aren't any lumps.

If you do the mixer macaronage, make sure you start at a low to medium speed – never crank it up to the highest setting! I'd recommend timing how long it takes. For me, it varies from 20-30 seconds. For you, it might be as low as 7 seconds to as high as 40 seconds. Batters that contain powdered ingredients such as cocoa or tea, usually take a few seconds longer to mix.

Ingredients:
- 160 grams powdered sugar, sift with almond flour
- 160 grams almond flour, sift with powdered sugar
- 150 grams egg whites
- 180 grams confectioners' sugar, sieved
- 1 Tablespoon [8 grams] arrowroot powder
- 1/2 teaspoon [3 grams] cream of tartar

Oven temperature: 300 degrees Fahrenheit/150 Celsius

Equipment:
- Stand or hand mixer with whisk and paddle attachments
- 2 – 4 large baking sheets
- Parchment paper or silicone mats
- Paper macaron template

- Large sieve or flour sifter
- Pastry/piping bag with large round tip
- Measuring cups/spoons/stainless steel or glass bowls
- Silicone or rubber spatula
- Large cup to hold piping bag
- Cooling rack
- Storage containers

Directions:

Preheat oven to 300 Fahrenheit/150 Celsius.

Sift the almond flour and confectioners' sugar together into a bowl. Stir in the arrowroot powder and set aside.

Put a template on a baking sheet and place a silicone mat or parchment paper over it. Set aside.

In the bowl of a stand mixer, add egg whites and confectioners' sugar. Whisk until well combined.

Place bowl over steaming pot with just enough water, as you don't want the water touching the bowl. Heat on medium until it steams. Test to make sure it's hot enough by sticking your clean finger in the meringue near the center of the bowl. If using a candy thermometer the temperature should be about 130 F [54 C].

Remove from heat and place bowl onto stand mixer. Add the cream of tartar.

Whisk on medium to high speed until firm peaks form. Egg whites should be glossy and if you flip the bowl upside down, nothing will come out.

Add food coloring and whisk until the color is incorporated.

Remove the whisk and add the paddle attachment [if using one].

Add the presifted almond flour and confectioners' sugar mixture.

Turn mixer to low or medium speed and mix for up to 10 seconds. If that doesn't mix the batter thoroughly, mix for another 10 seconds. Turn off mixer and with your spatula, run it around the sides and bottom of bowl to make sure all the dry ingredients are incorporated.

Test for the ribbon stage. When you lift your spatula above the bowl, the batter should fall back to the bowl as one continuous stream and create a ribbon pattern.

Pour batter into a large pastry bag fitted with a large round tip.

Pipe onto the silicone or parchment covered baking sheets.

When finished with each sheet, bang baking sheet on counter to remove air bubbles. If you see any air bubbles, pop them with a toothpick.

Let shells rest on a flat surface in a cool, dry area for about 30 minutes. The surface will change from glossy to matte. To make sure they're done, gently touch the edge of one with your finger. There should be no trace of batter on your finger.

Bake for 15-20 minutes. This will vary depending on your oven. Carefully monitor the baking process and check your oven thermometer. After 8 or so minutes, rotate the tray to ensure even baking.

Macarons are done when you peel back the mat or the parchment paper and the shells don't stick.

Remove from oven and gently slide the parchment or silicone mat onto a cooling rack. The shells should be cool enough to remove after 10 minutes.

Place macaron shells on a wax paper covered baking sheet or tray for filling. Match similar sized shells together. Pipe the filling on the flat side of one shell and gently place the second shell on top.

Almond Macarons

This is a classic flavor and the filling also contains almond flour. Using a high quality almond extract will make the flavor even richer.

Ingredients:

- 160 grams powdered sugar, sift with almond flour
- 160 grams almond flour, sift with powdered sugar
- 150 grams egg whites
- 180 grams confectioners' sugar, sieved
- 1 Tablespoon [8 grams] arrowroot powder
- 2 teaspoons vanilla bean paste
- 1/2 teaspoon [3 grams] cream of tartar
- Sky blue gel food colorant

Instructions:

Preheat oven to 300 Fahrenheit/150 Celsius.

Sift the almond flour and confectioners' sugar together into a bowl. Stir in the arrowroot powder and set aside.

Put a template on a baking sheet and place a silicone mat or parchment paper over it. Set aside.

In the bowl of a stand mixer, add egg whites and confectioners' sugar. Whisk until well combined.

Place bowl over pot with just enough water, as you don't want the water touching the bowl. Heat on medium until meringue is hot. Test to make sure it's hot enough by sticking your clean finger in the meringue near the center of the bowl. If using a candy thermometer the temperature should be about 130 F [54 C].

Remove from heat and place bowl onto stand mixer. Add the cream of tartar and vanilla bean paste.

Whisk on medium to high speed until firm peaks form. Egg whites should be glossy and if you flip the bowl upside down, nothing will come out.

Add food coloring and whisk until the color is incorporated.

Remove the whisk and add the paddle attachment [if using one].

Add the presifted almond flour and confectioners' sugar mixture.

Turn mixer on low or medium speed and mix for up to 10 seconds. If that doesn't mix the batter thoroughly, mix for another 10 seconds. Turn off mixer and with your spatula, run it around the sides and bottom of bowl to make sure all the dry ingredients are incorporated.

Test for the ribbon stage. When you lift your spatula above the bowl, the batter should fall back to the bowl as one continuous stream and create a ribbon pattern.

Pour batter into a pastry bag [14" or 16"] fitted with a large round tip.

Pipe onto the silicone or parchment covered baking sheets.

When finished with each sheet, bang baking sheet on counter to remove air bubbles. If you see any air bubbles, pop them with a toothpick.

Let shells rest on a flat surface in a cool, dry area for about 30 minutes.

The surface will change from glossy to matte. To make sure they're done, gently touch the edge of one with your finger. There should be no trace of batter on your finger.

Bake for 15-20 minutes. This will vary depending on your oven. Carefully monitor the baking process and check your oven thermometer. After 8 or so minutes, rotate the tray to ensure even baking.

Macarons are done when you peel back the mat or the parchment paper and the shells don't stick.

Remove from oven and gently slide the parchment or silicone mat onto a cooling rack. The shells should be cool enough to remove after 10 minutes.

Place macaron shells on a wax paper covered baking sheet or tray for filling. Match similar sized shells together. Pipe the filling on the flat side of one shell and gently place the second shell on top.

Whipped Almond Buttercream Filling

This is a European type of filling as it contains almond flour for a thickener and for the taste and texture. For more texture, you can use unblanched almond flour.

Ingredients:
- 125 grams [4 ounces] butter, room temperature
- 86 grams [3 ounces] almond flour sifting isn't necessary
- 86 grams [3 ounces] confectioners' sugar, sifted
- 1 1/2 teaspoons vanilla bean paste
- 1 teaspoon almond extract

Instructions:
In a stand mixer with a whisk attachment, whip the butter on medium speed until smooth and creamy.

Add the powdered sugar, starting at low speed and gradually changing to medium speed. When thoroughly mixed add the almond flour and whisk until the filling is smooth and creamy.

Add the vanilla bean paste and almond extract.

Scoop into a piping bag, the use of a tip is optional.

Apple Spice Macarons

This is for people who love apples with a hint of spice. A great autumn macaron recipe.

Ingredients

- 160 grams powdered sugar, sift with almond flour
- 160 grams almond flour, sift with powdered sugar
- 150 grams egg whites
- 180 grams confectioners' sugar, sieved
- 1 Tablespoon [8 grams] arrowroot powder
- 1/2 teaspoon [3 grams] cream of tartar
- 1 teaspoon vanilla bean paste
- Burgundy gel food colorant

Instructions

Preheat oven to 300 Fahrenheit/150 Celsius.

Sift the almond flour and confectioners' sugar together into a bowl. Stir in the arrowroot powder and set aside.

Put a template on a baking sheet and place a silicone mat or parchment paper over it. Set aside.

In the bowl of a stand mixer, add egg whites and confectioners' sugar. Whisk until well combined.

Place bowl over pot with just enough water, as you don't want the water touching the bowl. Heat on medium until meringue is hot. Test to make sure it's hot enough by sticking your clean finger in the meringue near the center of the bowl. If using a candy thermometer the temperature should be about 130 F [54 C].

Remove from heat and place bowl onto stand mixer. Add the cream of tartar and vanilla bean paste.

Whisk on medium to high speed until firm peaks form. Egg whites should be glossy and if you flip the bowl upside down, nothing will come out.

Add food coloring and whisk until the color is incorporated.

Remove the whisk and add the paddle attachment [if using one].

Add the presifted almond flour and confectioners' sugar mixture.

Turn mixer on low or medium speed and mix for up to 10 seconds. If that doesn't mix the batter thoroughly, mix for another 10 seconds. Turn off mixer and with your spatula, run it around the sides and bottom of bowl to make sure all the dry ingredients are incorporated.

Test for the ribbon stage. When you lift your spatula above the bowl, the batter should fall back to the bowl as one continuous stream and create a ribbon pattern.

Pour batter into a pastry bag [14" or 16"] fitted with a large round tip.

Pipe onto the silicone or parchment covered baking sheets.

When finished with each sheet, bang baking sheet on counter to remove air bubbles. If you see any air bubbles, pop them with a toothpick.

Let shells rest on a flat surface in a cool, dry area for about 30 minutes.

The surface will change from glossy to matte. To make sure they're done, gently touch the edge of one with your finger. There should be no trace of batter on your finger.

Bake for 15-20 minutes. This will vary depending on your oven. Carefully monitor the baking process and check your oven thermometer. After 8 or so minutes, rotate the tray to ensure even baking.

Macarons are done when you peel back the mat or the parchment paper and the shells don't stick.

Remove from oven and gently slide the parchment or silicone mat onto a cooling rack. The shells should be cool enough to remove after 10 minutes.

Place macaron shells on a wax paper covered baking sheet or tray for filling. Match similar sized shells together. Pipe the filling on the flat side of one shell and gently place the second shell on top.

Apple Spice Buttercream Filling

Ingredients
- 115 grams [1/4 cup] apple butter
- 115 grams [1/4 cup] unsalted butter
- 150 grams [3/4 cup] dark brown sugar OR organic pure cane sugar
- 30 ml [2 Tablespoons] heavy [double] cream
- 2 teaspoons Apple Pie Spice*
- 125 grams [1 cup] confectioners' sugar, sifted

Instructions
Melt the butter in a saucepan, then add the apple butter and brown sugar. Bring to a boil and reduce heat to medium low. Continue to boil for 2 minutes, whisking constantly. Add the cream, apple pie spice and cinnamon, whisking constantly, and return to a boil. Remove from heat

and cool to room temperature. Whisk powdered sugar until smooth and it reaches a frosting consistency.

* Make your own Apple Pie Spice by combining: 1 1/2 teaspoon (3 grams) cinnamon, 1/2 teaspoon (2 grams) nutmeg, 1/4 teaspoon (1 gram) allspice and two dashes of cloves. Add ingredients to a small container and shake until blended.

Banana Coconut Macarons

Shopping for a fruity tropical taste of sweetness? This is a great combination for those who adore such a compatible flavor duo.

Ingredients

- 160 grams powdered sugar, sift with almond flour
- 160 grams almond flour, sift with powdered sugar
- 150 grams egg whites
- 185 grams confectioners' sugar, sieved
- 1 Tablespoon [8 grams] arrowroot powder
- 1/2 teaspoon [3 grams] cream of tartar
- Colorful sprinkles [optional]
- Yellow food gel

Instructions

Preheat oven to 300 Fahrenheit/150 Celsius.

Sift the almond flour and confectioners' sugar together into a bowl. Stir in the arrowroot powder and set aside.

Put a template on a baking sheet and place a silicone mat or parchment paper over it. Set aside.

In the bowl of a stand mixer, add egg whites and confectioners' sugar. Whisk until well combined.

Place bowl over pot with just enough water, as you don't want the water touching the bowl. Heat on medium until meringue is hot. Test to make sure it's hot enough by sticking your clean finger in the meringue near the center of the bowl. If using a candy thermometer the temperature should be about 130 F [54 C].

Remove from heat and place bowl onto stand mixer. Add the cream of tartar.

Whisk on medium to high speed until firm peaks form. Egg whites should be glossy and if you flip the bowl upside down, nothing will come out.

Add food coloring and whisk until the color is incorporated.

Remove the whisk and add the paddle attachment [if using one].

Add the presifted almond flour and confectioners' sugar mixture.

Turn mixer on low or medium speed and mix for up to 10 seconds. If that doesn't mix the batter thoroughly, mix for another 10 seconds. Turn off mixer and with your spatula, run it around the sides and bottom of bowl to make sure all the dry ingredients are incorporated.

Test for the ribbon stage. When you lift your spatula above the bowl, the batter should fall back to the bowl as one continuous stream and create a ribbon pattern.

Pour batter into a pastry bag [14" or 16"] fitted with a large round tip.

Pipe onto the silicone or parchment covered baking sheets.

When finished with each sheet, bang baking sheet on counter to remove air bubbles. If you see any air bubbles, pop them with a toothpick.

Add the sprinkles on top of the macaron shells.

Let shells rest on a flat surface in a cool, dry area for about 30 minutes. The surface will change from glossy to matte. To make sure they're done, gently touch the edge of one with your finger. There should be no trace of batter on your finger.

Bake for 15-20 minutes. This will vary depending on your oven. Carefully monitor the baking process and check your oven thermometer. After 8 or so minutes, rotate the tray to ensure even baking.

Macarons are done when you peel back the mat or the parchment paper and the shells don't stick.

Remove from oven and gently slide the parchment or silicone mat onto a cooling rack. The shells should be cool enough to remove after 10 minutes.

Place macaron shells on a wax paper covered baking sheet or tray for filling. Match similar sized shells together. Pipe the filling on the flat side of one shell and gently place the second shell on top.

Banana Coconut Filling

Ingredients
- 2 cups confectioners' sugar
- 1 cup unsalted butter, room temperature
- ½ cup cream cheese, room temperature
- 2 teaspoons vanilla bean paste
- 2 teaspoons banana extract
- 1 teaspoon coconut extract
- Yellow food gel

Instructions
Beat the butter and cream cheese until fluffy. Add the vanilla while continuing to beat. Sift in the powdered sugar through a sifter. Mix for several minutes. Add extracts. Spoon into a piping bag.

Chocolate Macarons

Although I love chocolate, I've never baked a great looking batch of chocolate macarons. When first learning how to bake them, I tried twice. One batch resembled brownies and the other batch had different problems. Some bakers claim that chocolate macarons are easy but my experience has led me to believe otherwise. Adding any powdered ingredient to the shells can change the outcome of the cookies. Too much cocoa powder can and will darken your shells and increase your macaronage time. You'll also need to bake them for a couple of minutes longer and at a higher temperature setting. I increased my oven temperature by five degrees.

Ingredients

- 160 grams powdered sugar, sift with almond flour
- 160 grams almond flour, sift with powdered sugar
- 150 grams egg whites
- 180 grams confectioners' sugar, sieved
- 2 teaspoons cocoa powder, sifted*
- 1 Tablespoon [8 grams] arrowroot powder
- 1/2 teaspoon [3 grams] cream of tartar

- Brown gel food colorant

Instructions

Preheat oven to 305 Fahrenheit/150 Celsius.

Sift the almond flour, confectioners' sugar and cocoa powder together into a bowl. Stir in the arrowroot powder and set aside.

Put a template on a baking sheet and place a silicone mat or parchment paper over it. Set aside.

In the bowl of a stand mixer, add egg whites and confectioners' sugar. Whisk until well combined.

Place bowl over pot with just enough water, as you don't want the water touching the bowl. Heat on medium until meringue is hot. Test to make sure it's hot enough by sticking your clean finger in the meringue near the center of the bowl. If using a candy thermometer the temperature should be about 130 F [54 C].

Remove from heat and place bowl onto stand mixer. Add the cream of tartar.

Whisk on medium to high speed until firm peaks form. Egg whites should be glossy and if you flip the bowl upside down, nothing will come out.

Add food coloring and whisk until the color is incorporated.

Remove the whisk and add the paddle attachment [if using one].

Add the presifted almond flour and confectioners' sugar mixture.

Turn mixer on low or medium speed and mix for up to 10 seconds. If that doesn't mix the batter thoroughly, mix for another 10 seconds. Turn off mixer and with your spatula, run it around the sides and bottom of bowl to make sure all the dry ingredients are incorporated.

Test for the ribbon stage. When you lift your spatula above the bowl, the batter should fall back to the bowl as one continuous stream and create a ribbon pattern.

Pour batter into a pastry bag [14" or 16"] fitted with a large round tip.

Pipe onto the silicone or parchment covered baking sheets.

When finished with each sheet, bang baking sheet on counter to remove air bubbles. If you see any air bubbles, pop them with a toothpick.

Let shells rest on a flat surface in a cool, dry area for about 30 minutes. The surface will change from glossy to matte. To make sure they're done, gently touch the edge of one with your finger. There should be no trace of batter on your finger.

Bake for 15-20 minutes. This will vary depending on your oven. Carefully monitor the baking process and check your oven thermometer. After 8 or so minutes, rotate the tray to ensure even baking.

Macarons are done when you peel back the mat or the parchment paper and the shells don't stick.

Remove from oven and gently slide the parchment or silicone mat onto a cooling rack. The shells should be cool enough to remove after 10 minutes.

Place macaron shells on a wax paper covered baking sheet or tray for filling. Match similar sized shells together. Pipe the filling on the flat side of one shell and gently place the second shell on top.

*Even macaron shells containing a small amount of cocoa powder need to bake at a slightly higher heat and for a little longer than usual.

Chocolate Coconut Ganache Filling
[vegan/non-dairy]

Ingredients

- 10 ounces dark chocolate, chopped
- 5.46 ounces unsweetened coconut milk [1 small can]
- 1 Tablespoon virgin coconut oil
- 1-2 teaspoons coconut flavor or extract

Instructions

Before opening the can of coconut milk, shake well. Place in a microwave-safe container. Heat until just starting to simmer, approximately one minute. Pour over chocolate. Add virgin coconut oil and let sit for a few minutes as the chocolate melts. Stir to combine.

Add coconut extract or flavor and whisk until fully incorporated. Let cool until thick but not hard.

Scoop into a piping bag.

Chocolate & Red Fruit Macarons

These are decadently delicious chocolate macarons with a fruity and slightly tart fruit filling. The red fruit jam I used contained strawberries, cherries, redcurrants, and raspberries. Depending on your taste or what's on hand, you can use any type of red fruit[s] to incorporate into your chocolate ganache.

Ingredients
- 160 grams powdered sugar, sift with almond flour
- 155 grams almond flour, sift with powdered sugar
- 150 grams egg whites
- 180 grams confectioners' sugar, sieved
- 5 grams [2 teaspoons] cocoa powder, sieved
- 1 Tablespoon [8 grams] arrowroot powder
- 1/2 teaspoon [3 grams] cream of tartar
- Brown gel food colorant
- Colorful sprinkles [optional]

Instructions

Preheat oven to 305 Fahrenheit/150 Celsius.

Sift the almond flour, confectioners' sugar, and cocoa powder into a bowl. Stir in the arrowroot powder and set aside.

Put a template on a baking sheet and place a silicone mat or parchment paper over it. Set aside.

In the bowl of a stand mixer, add egg whites and confectioners' sugar. Whisk until well combined.

Place bowl over steaming pot with just enough water, as you don't want the water touching the bowl. Heat on medium heat until it steams. Test to make sure it's hot enough by sticking your clean finger in the meringue near the center of the bowl. If using a candy thermometer the temperature should be about 130 F [54 C].

Remove from heat and place bowl back onto stand mixer. Add the cream of tartar.

Whisk on medium to high speed until firm peaks form. Egg whites should be glossy and if you flip the bowl upside down, nothing will come out.

Add food coloring and whisk until the color is incorporated.

Remove the whisk and add the paddle attachment [if using one].

Add the presifted almond flour and confectioners' sugar mixture.

Turn mixer to low or medium speed and mix for up to 10 seconds. If that doesn't mix the batter thoroughly, mix for another 10 seconds. Turn off mixer and with your spatula, run it around the sides and bottom of bowl to make sure all the dry ingredients are incorporated.

Test for the ribbon stage. When you lift your spatula above the bowl, the batter should fall back to the bowl as one continuous stream and create a ribbon pattern.

Pour batter into a large pastry bag fitted with a large round tip.

Pipe onto the silicone or parchment covered baking sheets.

When finished with each sheet, bang baking sheet on counter to remove air bubbles. If you see any air bubbles, pop them with a toothpick.

Sprinkle the colorful sprinkles on top of the macaron shells.

Let shells rest on a flat surface in a cool, dry area for about 30 minutes. The surface will change from glossy to matte. To make sure they're done, gently touch the edge of one with your finger. There should be no trace of batter on your finger.

Bake for 15-22 minutes. This will vary depending on your oven. Carefully monitor the baking process and check your oven thermometer. After 8 or so minutes, rotate the tray to ensure even baking.

Macarons are done when you peel back the mat or the parchment paper and the shells don't stick.

Remove from oven and gently slide the parchment or silicone mat onto a cooling rack. The shells should be cool enough to remove after 10 minutes.

Place macaron shells on a wax paper covered baking sheet or tray for filling. Match similar sized shells together. Pipe the filling on the flat side of one shell and gently place the second shell on top.

Chocolate & Red Fruit Ganache

Ingredients
- 118 ml [4 ounces] heavy [double] cream
- 120 grams [4 ounces] finely chopped dark chocolate
- 60 ml [1/4 cup] red fruit jam

Instructions

In a small bowl over a pot of simmering water, melt the chopped chocolate. When melted, add the cream, and jam. Stir well. Store in a plastic-wrap covered bowl overnight. Spoon into a piping bag with no tip.

Cinnamon Roll Macarons

For cinnamon lovers. Whether you adore cinnamon during the Christmas season or any time of the year, these sweet and spicy macarons are sure to please.

Ingredients

- 160 grams powdered sugar, sift with almond flour
- 160 grams almond flour, sift with powdered sugar
- 150 grams egg whites
- 180 grams confectioners' sugar, sieved
- 1 Tablespoon [8 grams] arrowroot powder
- 1/2 teaspoon [3 grams] cream of tartar
- 1/2 teaspoon [3 grams] ground cinnamon
- 1/2 teaspoon vanilla bean paste
- Brown edible food color pen

Instructions

Preheat oven to 300 Fahrenheit/150 Celsius.

Sift the almond flour and confectioners' sugar together into a bowl. Stir in the arrowroot powder and cinnamon, and set aside.

Put a template on a baking sheet and place a silicone mat or parchment paper over it. Set aside.

In the bowl of a stand mixer, add egg whites and confectioners' sugar. Whisk until well combined.

Place bowl over steaming pot with just enough water, as you don't want the water touching the bowl. Heat on medium heat until it steams. Test to make sure it's hot enough by sticking your clean finger in the meringue near the center of the bowl. If using a candy thermometer the temperature should be about 130 F [54 C].

Remove from heat and place bowl back onto stand mixer. Add the cream of tartar.

Whisk on medium to high speed until firm peaks form. Egg whites should be glossy and if you flip the bowl upside down, nothing will come out.

Add vanilla bean paste and whisk for a few seconds.

Remove the whisk and add the paddle attachment [if using one].

Add the presifted almond flour and confectioners' sugar mixture.

Turn mixer to low or medium speed and mix for up to 10 seconds. If that doesn't mix the batter thoroughly, mix for another 10 seconds. Turn off mixer and with your spatula, run it around the sides and bottom of bowl to make sure all the dry ingredients are incorporated.

Test for the ribbon stage. When you lift your spatula above the bowl, the batter should fall back to the bowl as one continuous stream and create a ribbon pattern.

Pour batter into a large pastry bag fitted with a large round tip.

Pipe onto the silicone or parchment covered baking sheets.

When finished with each sheet, bang baking sheet on counter to remove air bubbles. If you see any air bubbles, pop them with a toothpick.

Let shells rest on a flat surface in a cool, dry area for about 30 minutes. The surface will change from glossy to matte. To make sure they're done, gently touch the edge of one with your finger. There should be no trace of batter on your finger.

Bake for 15-20 minutes. This will vary depending on your oven. Carefully monitor the baking process and check your oven thermometer. After 8 or so minutes, rotate the tray to ensure even baking.

Macarons are done when you peel back the mat or the parchment paper and the shells don't stick.

Remove from oven and gently slide the parchment or silicone mat onto a cooling rack. The shells should be cool enough to remove after 10 minutes.

Place macaron shells on a wax paper covered baking sheet or tray for filling.

Using an edible brown food color gel pen, carefully draw spirals on each shell.

When the shells are dry, match similar sized shells together. Pipe the filling on the flat side of one shell and gently place the second shell on top.

Cinnamon Roll Filling

Ingredients
- 125 grams [4 ounces] unsalted butter, room temperature
- 125 grams [4 ounces] cream cheese, room temperature
- 220 grams [2 cups] confectioners' sugar, sifted
- 1 teaspoon vanilla bean paste
- 30 ml [2 Tablespoons] heavy [double] cream
- 1/2 teaspoon ground cinnamon

Instructions

In the bowl of a mixer/stand mixer, mix butter and cream cheese until well blended. Add the vanilla, heavy cream, and cinnamon. Continue to blend until well incorporated. Add the sugar and mix on high speed for a few minutes. Spoon into a piping bag and fill your macarons.

Cookie Butter [Speculoos] Macarons

You can find cookie butter online or at Trader Joe's. The gingery taste is different from peanut butter, although it certainly resembles it in color and texture. Cookie butter can be found in smooth or crunchy textures, along with variations that include swirls of cocoa, and cookies and crème.

Ingredients

- 160 grams powdered sugar, sift with almond flour
- 160 grams almond flour, sift with powdered sugar
- 150 grams egg whites
- 180 grams confectioners' sugar, sieved
- 1 Tablespoon [8 grams] Pumpkin Pie spice* seasoning for sprinkling
- 1 Tablespoon [8 grams] arrowroot powder
- 1/2 teaspoon [3 grams] cream of tartar
- Orange gel food colorant

Instructions

Preheat oven to 300 Fahrenheit/150 Celsius.

Sift the almond flour and confectioners' sugar together into a bowl. Stir in the arrowroot powder and set aside.

Put a template on a baking sheet and place a silicone mat or parchment paper over it. Set aside.

In the bowl of a stand mixer, add egg whites and confectioners' sugar. Whisk until well combined.

Place bowl over pot with just enough water, as you don't want the water touching the bowl. Heat on medium until meringue is hot. Test to make sure it's hot enough by sticking your clean finger in the meringue near the center of the bowl. If using a candy thermometer the temperature should be about 130 F [54 C].

Remove from heat and place bowl onto stand mixer. Add the cream of tartar.

Whisk on medium to high speed until firm peaks form. Egg whites should be glossy and if you flip the bowl upside down, nothing will come out.

Add food coloring and whisk until the color is incorporated.

Remove the whisk and add the paddle attachment [if using one].

Add the presifted almond flour and confectioners' sugar mixture.

Turn mixer on low or medium speed and mix for up to 10 seconds. If that doesn't mix the batter thoroughly, mix for another 10 seconds. Turn off mixer and with your spatula, run it around the sides and bottom of bowl to make sure all the dry ingredients are incorporated.

Test for the ribbon stage. When you lift your spatula above the bowl, the batter should fall back to the bowl as one continuous stream and create a ribbon pattern.

Pour batter into a pastry bag [14" or 16"] fitted with a large round tip.

Pipe onto the silicone or parchment covered baking sheets.

When finished with each sheet, bang baking sheet on counter to

remove air bubbles. If you see any air bubbles, pop them with a toothpick.

Sprinkle pumpkin pie spice seasoning over the shells.

Let shells rest on a flat surface in a cool, dry area for about 30 minutes. The surface will change from glossy to matte. To make sure they're done, gently touch the edge of one with your finger. There should be no trace of batter on your finger.

Bake for 15-20 minutes. This will vary depending on your oven. Carefully monitor the baking process and check your oven thermometer. After 8 or so minutes, rotate the tray to ensure even baking.

Macarons are done when you peel back the mat or the parchment paper and the shells don't stick.

Remove from oven and gently slide the parchment or silicone mat onto a cooling rack. The shells should be cool enough to remove after 10 minutes.

Place macaron shells on a wax paper covered baking sheet or tray for filling. Match similar sized shells together. Pipe the filling on the flat side of one shell and gently place the second shell on top.

Cookie Butter Filling

Just put cookie butter into a piping bag with no tip and you're ready to pipe.

- Pumpkin Pie Spice blend
- 1 Tablespoon [8 grams] ground cinnamon
- 2 teaspoons ground ginger
- 1/2 teaspoon [3 grams] allspice
- 1/2 teaspoon [3 grams] ground cloves
- 1/2 teaspoon [3 grams] ground nutmeg

Dark Chocolate & Butterscotch Macarons

Since butterscotch is so sweet, I opted to use an 85% dark chocolate to balance it. Making two different ganaches is a little more work but if you're a fan of this lovely combination you won't mind! I used Guittard butterscotch baking chips—a brand I highly recommend.

Ingredients
- 160 grams powdered sugar, sift with almond flour
- 160 grams almond flour, sift with powdered sugar
- 150 grams egg whites
- 180 grams confectioners' sugar, sieved
- 2 teaspoons [5 grams] cocoa powder, sieved
- 1 Tablespoon [8 grams] arrowroot powder
- 1/2 teaspoon [3 grams] cream of tartar
- Brown gel food colorant

Instructions
Preheat oven to 305 Fahrenheit/150 Celsius.

Sift the almond flour, confectioners' sugar and cocoa powder together into a bowl. Stir in the arrowroot powder and set aside.

Put a template on a baking sheet and place a silicone mat or parchment paper over it. Set aside.

In the bowl of a stand mixer, add egg whites and confectioners' sugar. Whisk until well combined.

Place bowl over steaming pot with just enough water, as you don't want the water touching the bowl. Heat on medium heat until it steams. Test to make sure it's hot enough by sticking your clean finger in the meringue near the center of the bowl. If using a candy thermometer the temperature should be about 130 F [54 C].

Remove from heat and place bowl back onto stand mixer. Add the cream of tartar.

Whisk on medium to high speed until firm peaks form. Egg whites should be glossy and if you flip the bowl upside down, nothing will come out.

Add food coloring and whisk until the color is incorporated.

Remove the whisk and add the paddle attachment [if using one].

Add the presifted almond flour and confectioners' sugar mixture.

Turn mixer to low or medium speed and mix for up to 10 seconds. If that doesn't mix the batter thoroughly, mix for another 10 seconds. Turn off mixer and with your spatula, run it around the sides and bottom of bowl to make sure all the dry ingredients are incorporated.

Test for the ribbon stage. When you lift your spatula above the bowl, the batter should fall back to the bowl as one continuous stream and create a ribbon pattern.

Pour batter into a large pastry bag fitted with a large round tip.

Pipe onto the silicone or parchment covered baking sheets.

When finished with each sheet, bang baking sheet on counter to

remove air bubbles. If you see any air bubbles, pop them with a toothpick.

Let shells rest on a flat surface in a cool, dry area for about 30 minutes. The surface will change from glossy to matte. To make sure they're done, gently touch the edge of one with your finger. There should be no trace of batter on your finger.

Bake for 15-20 minutes. This will vary depending on your oven. Carefully monitor the baking process and check your oven thermometer. After 8 or so minutes, rotate the tray to ensure even baking.

Macarons are done when you peel back the mat or the parchment paper and the shells don't stick.

Remove from oven and gently slide the parchment or silicone mat onto a cooling rack. The shells should be cool enough to remove after 10 minutes.

Place macaron shells on a wax paper covered baking sheet or tray for filling. Match similar sized shells together. Pipe the filling on the flat side of one shell and gently place the second shell on top.

Chocolate Ganache Filling

Ingredients
- 118 ml [4 ounces] heavy [double] cream
- 120 grams [4 ounces] finely chopped dark chocolate, 85% cacao
- 1 teaspoon vanilla extract or vanilla bean paste

Instructions
Place heavy cream in a microwave-safe container. Heat until just starting to simmer, approximately one minute. Pour over chocolate. Add vanilla and let sit for a few minutes as the chocolate melts. Stir to combine.

Let cool until thick but not hard.

Scoop into a piping bag.

Butterscotch Ganache Filling

Ingredients

- 6 ounces [170 grams] butterscotch morsels
- 60 ml. [4 Tablespoons] heavy [double] cream
- 30 grams [2 Tablespoons] unsalted butter
- 1-2 teaspoons vanilla bean paste

Instructions

In a small bowl over a pot of simmering water, melt the butterscotch morsels. When they've melted, add the cream, butter and vanilla bean paste. Stir well. Let cool until thick but not hard. Scoop into a piping bag.

Festive Cereal Macarons

If you can't find *Oops! All Berries* cereal, you can use a different brand or type of cereal. The brighter the colors, the more festive looking the macarons!

Ingredients

- 160 grams powdered sugar, sift with almond flour
- 160 grams almond flour, sift with powdered sugar
- 150 grams egg whites
- 180 grams confectioners' sugar, sieved
- 2 Tablespoons *Oops! All Berries* cereal, crushed
- 1 Tablespoon [8 grams] arrowroot powder
- 1/2 teaspoon [3 grams] cream of tartar
- Electric pink gel food colorant

Instructions

Preheat oven to 300 Fahrenheit/150 Celsius.

Sift the almond flour and confectioners' sugar together into a bowl. Stir in the arrowroot powder and set aside.

Put a template on a baking sheet and place a silicone mat or parchment

paper over it. Set aside.

In the bowl of a stand mixer, add egg whites and confectioners' sugar. Whisk until well combined.

Place bowl over pot with just enough water, as you don't want the water touching the bowl. Heat on medium until meringue is hot. Test to make sure it's hot enough by sticking your clean finger in the meringue near the center of the bowl. If using a candy thermometer the temperature should be about 130 F [54 C].

Remove from heat and place bowl onto stand mixer. Add the cream of tartar.

Whisk on medium to high speed until firm peaks form. Egg whites should be glossy and if you flip the bowl upside down, nothing will come out.

Add food coloring and whisk until the color is incorporated.

Remove the whisk and add the paddle attachment [if using one].

Add the presifted almond flour and confectioners' sugar mixture.

Turn mixer on low or medium speed and mix for up to 10 seconds. If that doesn't mix the batter thoroughly, mix for another 10 seconds. Turn off mixer and with your spatula, run it around the sides and bottom of bowl to make sure all the dry ingredients are incorporated.

Test for the ribbon stage. When you lift your spatula above the bowl, the batter should fall back to the bowl as one continuous stream and create a ribbon pattern.

Pour batter into a pastry bag [14" or 16"] fitted with a large round tip.

Pipe onto the silicone or parchment covered baking sheets.

When finished with each sheet, bang baking sheet on counter to remove air bubbles. If you see any air bubbles, pop them with a toothpick.

Sprinkle the crushed *Oops! All Berries* on top of the shells.

Let shells rest on a flat surface in a cool, dry area for about 30 minutes. The surface will change from glossy to matte. To make sure they're done, gently touch the edge of one with your finger. There should be no trace of batter on your finger.

Bake for 15-20 minutes. This will vary depending on your oven. Carefully monitor the baking process and check your oven thermometer. After 8 or so minutes, rotate the tray to ensure even baking.

Macarons are done when you peel back the mat or the parchment paper and the shells don't stick.

Remove from oven and gently slide the parchment or silicone mat onto a cooling rack. The shells should be cool enough to remove after 10 minutes.

Place macaron shells on a wax paper covered baking sheet or tray for filling. Match similar sized shells together. Pipe the filling on the flat side of one shell and gently place the second shell on top.

Festive Cereal Buttercream Filling

Ingredients
- 85 grams [3 ounces] cream cheese, room temperature
- 85 grams [3 ounces], butter, room temperature
- 250 grams [2 cups] confectioners' sugar, sifted
- 15 ml [1 Tablespoon] heavy cream
- 1 teaspoon vanilla
- 15 grams [1/2 cup] crushed All Berries
- Turquoise gel food color

Instructions
Place the softened cream cheese and butter into a mixing bowl and mix on high speed for several minutes until creamy. Slowly add in the

confectioners' sugar, vanilla, and heavy cream. Mix in the crushed berries. If needed, add turquoise food color. Lastly, add the whole berries and mix for a few seconds until they're incorporated.

Scoop into a piping bag.

Fig, Mascarpone & Honey Macarons

The creamy filling contains Italian mascarpone, and this filling contains less sugar to sweeten it.

Ingredients

- 160 grams powdered sugar, sift with almond flour
- 160 grams almond flour, sift with powdered sugar
- 150 grams egg whites
- 180 grams confectioners' sugar, sieved
- 1 Tablespoon [8 grams] arrowroot powder
- 1/2 teaspoon [3 grams] cream of tartar
- 2 Tablespoons [16 grams] finely crushed walnuts
- Forest green food gel

Instructions

Preheat oven to 300 Fahrenheit/150 Celsius.

Sift the almond flour and confectioners' sugar together into a bowl. Stir in the arrowroot powder and set aside.

Put a template on a baking sheet and place a silicone mat or parchment paper over it. Set aside.

In the bowl of a stand mixer, add egg whites and confectioners' sugar. Whisk until well combined.

Place bowl over steaming pot with just enough water, as you don't want the water touching the bowl. Heat on medium heat until it steams. Test to make sure it's hot enough by sticking your clean finger in the meringue near the center of the bowl. If using a candy thermometer the temperature should be about 130 F [54 C].

Remove from heat and place bowl back onto stand mixer. Add the cream of tartar.

Whisk on medium to high speed until firm peaks form. Egg whites should be glossy and if you flip the bowl upside down, nothing will come out.

Add food coloring and whisk until the color is incorporated.

Remove the whisk and add the paddle attachment [if using one].

Add the presifted almond flour and confectioners' sugar mixture.

Turn mixer to low or medium speed and mix for up to 10 seconds. If that doesn't mix the batter thoroughly, mix for another 10 seconds. Turn off mixer and with your spatula, run it around the sides and bottom of bowl to make sure all the dry ingredients are incorporated.

Test for the ribbon stage. When you lift your spatula above the bowl, the batter should fall back to the bowl as one continuous stream and create a ribbon pattern.

Pour batter into a large pastry bag fitted with a large round tip.

Pipe onto the silicone or parchment covered baking sheets.

When finished with each sheet, bang baking sheet on counter to remove air bubbles. If you see any air bubbles, pop them with a toothpick.

Sprinkle crushed walnuts on the macaron shells.

Let shells rest on a flat surface in a cool, dry area for about 30 minutes.

The surface will change from glossy to matte. To make sure they're done, gently touch the edge of one with your finger. There should be no trace of batter on your finger.

Bake for 15-20 minutes. This will vary depending on your oven. Carefully monitor the baking process and check your oven thermometer. After 8 or so minutes, rotate the tray to ensure even baking.

Macarons are done when you peel back the mat or the parchment paper and the shells don't stick.

Remove from oven and gently slide the parchment or silicone mat onto a cooling rack. The shells should be cool enough to remove after 10 minutes.

Place macaron shells on a wax paper covered baking sheet or tray for filling. Match similar sized shells together. Pipe the filling on the flat side of one shell and gently place the second shell on top.

Fig, Honey & Mascarpone Filling

Ingredients

- 125 grams [4 ounces] unsalted butter, room temperature
- 125 grams [4 ounces] mascarpone cheese, room temperature
- 40 grams [heaping 1/3 cup] confectioners' sugar, sifted
- 1 Tablespoon honey
- 1 teaspoon vanilla bean paste
- 60 ml [1/4 cup] fig jam or fig spread
- Bright pink food gel color

Instructions

In the bowl of a stand mixer, mix mascarpone and butter together for a few minutes. When well incorporated, add the vanilla, honey, fig jam, and confectioners' sugar. Mix for a few minutes and add the colorant. Spoon into a piping bag.

Froot Loops Macarons

This is for fans of Froot Loops or similar types of sweet and colorful cereal.

Ingredients

- 160 grams powdered sugar, sift with almond flour
- 160 grams almond flour, sift with powdered sugar
- 150 grams egg whites
- 180 grams confectioners' sugar, sieved
- 2-3 Tablespoons crushed Froot Loops cereal for sprinkling
- 1 Tablespoon [8 grams] arrowroot powder
- 1/2 teaspoon [3 grams] cream of tartar
- Pink or purple gel food colorant

Instructions

Preheat oven to 300 Fahrenheit/150 Celsius.

Sift the almond flour and confectioners' sugar together into a bowl. Stir in the arrowroot powder and set aside.

Put a template on a baking sheet and place a silicone mat or parchment paper over it. Set aside.

In the bowl of a stand mixer, add egg whites and confectioners' sugar. Whisk until well combined.

Place bowl over steaming pot with just enough water, as you don't want the water touching the bowl. Heat on medium heat until it steams. Test to make sure it's hot enough by sticking your clean finger in the meringue near the center of the bowl. If using a candy thermometer the temperature should be about 130 F [54 C].

Remove from heat and place bowl back onto stand mixer. Add the cream of tartar.

Whisk on medium to high speed until firm peaks form. Egg whites should be glossy and if you flip the bowl upside down, nothing will come out.

Add food coloring and whisk until the color is incorporated.

Remove the whisk and add the paddle attachment [if using one].

Add the presifted almond flour and confectioners' sugar mixture.

Turn mixer to low or medium speed and mix for up to 10 seconds. If that doesn't mix the batter thoroughly, mix for another 10 seconds. Turn off mixer and with your spatula, run it around the sides and bottom of bowl to make sure all the dry ingredients are incorporated.

Test for the ribbon stage. When you lift your spatula above the bowl, the batter should fall back to the bowl as one continuous stream and create a ribbon pattern.

Pour batter into a large pastry bag fitted with a large round tip.

Pipe onto the silicone or parchment covered baking sheets.

When finished with each sheet, bang baking sheet on counter to remove air bubbles. If you see any air bubbles, pop them with a toothpick.

Sprinkle crushed Froot Loops on the macaron shells

Let shells rest on a flat surface in a cool, dry area for about 30 minutes.

The surface will change from glossy to matte. To make sure they're done, gently touch the edge of one with your finger. There should be no trace of batter on your finger.

Bake for 15-20 minutes. This will vary depending on your oven. Carefully monitor the baking process and check your oven thermometer. After 8 or so minutes, rotate the tray to ensure even baking.

Macarons are done when you peel back the mat or the parchment paper and the shells don't stick.

Remove from oven and gently slide the parchment or silicone mat onto a cooling rack. The shells should be cool enough to remove after 10 minutes.

Place macaron shells on a wax paper covered baking sheet or tray for filling. Match similar sized shells together. Pipe the filling on the flat side of one shell and gently place the second shell on top.

Froot Loops Ganache Filling

For a sweet and colorful macaron filling, this easy to make white chocolate ganache only takes a few minutes to prepare. If you want a slightly thicker version, just add a little more crushed cereal.

Ingredients
- 170 grams [6 ounces] white chocolate chunks
- 473 ml [2 cups] heavy [double] cream
- 15 grams [1/2 cup] crushed Froot Loops cereal

Instructions
Heat the heavy cream in a microwave until it's very hot but not boiling. Pour into the bowl of white chocolate chunks. Stir until smooth. Add the crushed Froot Loops, mixing until incorporated. Cover with cling wrap and put in the refrigerator for a couple of hours, until it's no longer runny. Spoon into a piping bag with no tip.

Key Lime Marmalade Macarons

You can substitute key lime jelly or jam for this recipe. I created this recipe for anyone who loves key lime pie, or as an alternative to the Oreo key lime macaron recipe.

Ingredients

- 160 grams powdered sugar, sift with almond flour
- 160 grams almond flour, sift with powdered sugar
- 150 grams egg whites
- 180 grams confectioners' sugar, sieved
- 1/2 teaspoon [3 grams] cream of tartar
- 2-3 Tablespoons crushed graham crackers
- Green food gel colorant

Instructions

Preheat oven to 300 Fahrenheit/150 Celsius.

Sift the almond flour and confectioners' sugar together into a bowl. Stir in the arrowroot powder and set aside.

Put a template on a baking sheet and place a silicone mat or parchment paper over it. Set aside.

In the bowl of a stand mixer, add egg whites and confectioners' sugar. Whisk until well combined.

Place bowl over pot with just enough water, as you don't want the water touching the bowl. Heat on medium until meringue is hot. Test to make sure it's hot enough by sticking your clean finger in the meringue near the center of the bowl. If using a candy thermometer the temperature should be about 130 F [54 C].

Remove from heat and place bowl onto stand mixer. Add the cream of tartar.

Whisk on medium to high speed until firm peaks form. Egg whites should be glossy and if you flip the bowl upside down, nothing will come out.

Add food coloring and whisk until the color is incorporated.

Remove the whisk and add the paddle attachment [if using one].

Add the presifted almond flour and confectioners' sugar mixture.

Turn mixer on low or medium speed and mix for up to 10 seconds. If that doesn't mix the batter thoroughly, mix for another 10 seconds. Turn off mixer and with your spatula, run it around the sides and bottom of bowl to make sure all the dry ingredients are incorporated.

Test for the ribbon stage. When you lift your spatula above the bowl, the batter should fall back to the bowl as one continuous stream and create a ribbon pattern.

Pour batter into a pastry bag [14" or 16"] fitted with a large round tip.

Pipe onto the silicone or parchment covered baking sheets.

When finished with each sheet, bang baking sheet on counter to remove air bubbles. If you see any air bubbles, pop them with a toothpick.

Sprinkle powdered graham cracker cookies over the macaron tops.

Let shells rest on a flat surface in a cool, dry area for about 30 minutes. The surface will change from glossy to matte. To make sure they're done, gently touch the edge of one with your finger. There should be no trace of batter on your finger.

Bake for 15-20 minutes. This will vary depending on your oven. Carefully monitor the baking process and check your oven thermometer. After 8 or so minutes, rotate the tray to ensure even baking.

Macarons are done when you peel back the mat or the parchment paper and the shells don't stick.

Remove from oven and gently slide the parchment or silicone mat onto a cooling rack. The shells should be cool enough to remove after 10 minutes.

Place macaron shells on a wax paper covered baking sheet or tray for filling. Match similar sized shells together. Pipe the filling on the flat side of one shell and gently place the second shell on top.

Key Lime Marmalade Buttercream Filling

Ingredients
- 115 grams [1/2 cup] butter, room temperature
- 60 ml [1/4 cup] key lime marmalade [or jam/jelly]
- 220 grams [2 cups] powdered sugar, sifted
- 1/2 Tablespoon heavy [double] cream
- 1 teaspoon vanilla
- Green gel food colorant

Instructions
Cream the butter until it's fluffy and slowly add powdered sugar until combined. Once well mixed, add the vanilla and key lime marmalade. Mix on high speed. Pour in the heavy cream and lastly add the green colorant.

Key Lime Pie Oreo Macarons

If you can find this special edition flavor of Oreo cookies in your store or online, then you can bake a lively tasting and looking macaron. If you can't get this brand, I've provided another type that looks and tastes just as good.

Ingredients

- 160 grams powdered sugar, sift with almond flour
- 160 grams almond flour, sift with powdered sugar
- 150 grams egg whites
- 180 grams confectioners' sugar, sieved
- 1 Tablespoon [8 grams] arrowroot powder
- 1/2 teaspoon [3 grams] cream of tartar
- Mint green gel food colorant
- 2-3 Tablespoons finely crushed graham cracker shells for sprinkling

Instructions

Preheat oven to 300 Fahrenheit/150 Celsius.

Sift the almond flour and confectioners' sugar together into a bowl. Stir in the arrowroot powder and set aside.

Put a template on a baking sheet and place a silicone mat or parchment paper over it. Set aside.

In the bowl of a stand mixer, add egg whites and confectioners' sugar. Whisk until well combined.

Place bowl over pot with just enough water, as you don't want the water touching the bowl. Heat on medium until meringue is hot. Test to make sure it's hot enough by sticking your clean finger in the meringue near the center of the bowl. If using a candy thermometer the temperature should be about 130 F [54 C].

Remove from heat and place bowl onto stand mixer. Add the cream of tartar.

Whisk on medium to high speed until firm peaks form. Egg whites should be glossy and if you flip the bowl upside down, nothing will come out.

Add food coloring and whisk until the color is incorporated.

Remove the whisk and add the paddle attachment [if using one].

Add the presifted almond flour and confectioners' sugar mixture.

Turn mixer on low or medium speed and mix for up to 10 seconds. If that doesn't mix the batter thoroughly, mix for another 10 seconds. Turn off mixer and with your spatula, run it around the sides and bottom of bowl to make sure all the dry ingredients are incorporated.

Test for the ribbon stage. When you lift your spatula above the bowl, the batter should fall back to the bowl as one continuous stream and create a ribbon pattern.

Pour batter into a pastry bag [14" or 16"] fitted with a large round tip.

Pipe onto the silicone or parchment covered baking sheets.

When finished with each sheet, bang baking sheet on counter to

remove air bubbles. If you see any air bubbles, pop them with a toothpick.

Sprinkle powdered graham cracker cookies over the macaron tops.

Let shells rest on a flat surface in a cool, dry area for about 30 minutes. The surface will change from glossy to matte. To make sure they're done, gently touch the edge of one with your finger. There should be no trace of batter on your finger.

Bake for 15-20 minutes. This will vary depending on your oven. Carefully monitor the baking process and check your oven thermometer. After 8 or so minutes, rotate the tray to ensure even baking.

Macarons are done when you peel back the mat or the parchment paper and the shells don't stick.

Remove from oven and gently slide the parchment or silicone mat onto a cooling rack. The shells should be cool enough to remove after 10 minutes.

Place macaron shells on a wax paper covered baking sheet or tray for filling. Match similar sized shells together. Pipe the filling on the flat side of one shell and gently place the second shell on top.

Key Lime Pie Oreo Graham Filling

Ingredients
- 60 grams [2.2 ounces] unsalted room temperature butter
- 100 grams [3.5 ounces] cream cheese
- 200 grams [2 cups] powdered sugar, sifted
- 18 Key Lime Pie Oreo Graham Filling cookies, separate filling and shells [finely crush shells]
- Mint green food color [optional]

Instructions

In a stand mixer with a paddle attachment, mix the butter and cream cheese until smooth and creamy.

Add the powdered sugar, starting at low speed and gradually changing to medium speed. When thoroughly mixed, add the cookie filling and mix until the filling is smooth and creamy.

Add a few tablespoons' worth of the crushed Oreo graham cracker shells.

If you want a brighter shade of green, add gel color.

Reserve the rest of the graham cracker shells to roll on the sides of your sandwiched macaron cookies.

Kiwi Swirl Macarons

Using fresh fruit that's in season is always the best option for a natural flavor. Paired with tri-colored shells, this method is fun and easy to do and your macarons will stand out.

Ingredients
- 160 grams powdered sugar, sift with almond flour
- 160 grams almond flour, sift with powdered sugar
- 150 grams egg whites
- 180 grams confectioners' sugar, sieved
- 1 Tablespoon [8 grams] arrowroot powder
- 1/2 teaspoon [3 grams] cream of tartar
- Forest green, mint & avocado gels for painting piping bag

Instructions
Preheat oven to 300 Fahrenheit/150 Celsius.

Sift the almond flour and confectioners' sugar together into a bowl. Stir in the arrowroot powder and set aside.

Put a template on a baking sheet and place a silicone mat or parchment paper over it. Set aside.

In the bowl of a stand mixer, add egg whites and confectioners' sugar. Whisk until well combined.

Place bowl over steaming pot with just enough water, as you don't want the water touching the bowl. Heat on medium until it steams. Test to make sure it's hot enough by sticking your clean finger in the meringue near the center of the bowl. If using a candy thermometer the temperature should be about 130 F [54 C].

Remove from heat and place bowl onto stand mixer. Add the cream of tartar.

Whisk on medium to high speed until firm peaks form. Egg whites should be glossy and if you flip the bowl upside down, nothing will come out.

While your meringue is mixing, paint the inside of the piping bag with the gel colorants. You can use one shade of green or a few different shades.

Remove the whisk and add the paddle attachment [if using one].

Add the presifted almond flour and confectioners' sugar mixture.

Turn mixer to low or medium speed and mix for up to 10 seconds. If that doesn't mix the batter thoroughly, mix for another 10 seconds. Turn off mixer and with your spatula, run it around the sides and bottom of bowl to make sure all the dry ingredients are incorporated.

Test for the ribbon stage. When you lift your spatula above the bowl, the batter should fall back to the bowl as one continuous stream and create a ribbon pattern.

Pour batter into a large pastry bag fitted with a large round tip.

Pipe onto the silicone or parchment covered baking sheets.

When finished with each sheet, bang baking sheet on counter to remove air bubbles. If you see any air bubbles, pop them with a toothpick.

Let shells rest on a flat surface in a cool, dry area for about 30 minutes. The surface will change from glossy to matte. To make sure they're done, gently touch the edge of one with your finger. There should be no trace of batter on your finger.

Bake for 15-20 minutes. This will vary depending on your oven. Carefully monitor the baking process and check your oven thermometer. After 8 or so minutes, rotate the tray to ensure even baking.

Macarons are done when you peel back the mat or the parchment paper and the shells don't stick.

Remove from oven and gently slide the parchment or silicone mat onto a cooling rack. The shells should be cool enough to remove after 10 minutes.

Place macaron shells on a wax paper covered baking sheet or tray for filling. Match similar sized shells together. Pipe the filling on the flat side of one shell and gently place the second shell on top.

Kiwi Mascarpone Filling

Ingredients
- 1 kiwi fruit, peeled and mashed
- 125 grams [4 ounces] unsalted butter, room temperature
- 125 grams [4 ounces] mascarpone cheese, room temperature
- 63 grams [1/2 cup] to 95 grams [3/4 cup] confectioners' sugar, sifted
- 1 Tablespoon honey
- 1 teaspoon vanilla
- 1 teaspoon cornstarch
- Avocado green food color gel

Instructions
In the bowl of a mixer/stand mixer, mix butter and mascarpone until

well blended. Add the honey and vanilla. Then add the kiwi fruit. Continue to blend until well incorporated. Add the sugar and mix on high speed for a few minutes. If the mixture is too loose, add the cornstarch. For a greener color, add green food gel. Scoop into a piping bag.

Lemon Chia Seed Macarons

For lovers of lemon. I used an electric yellow colorant to achieve such bright shells. The chia seeds are a healthy additive and the lemon ganache is sweet and tangy.

Ingredients

- 160 grams powdered sugar, sift with almond flour
- 160 grams almond flour, sift with powdered sugar
- 150 grams egg whites
- 180 grams confectioners' sugar, sieved
- 1-2 Tablespoons chia seeds for sprinkling
- 1 Tablespoon [8 grams] arrowroot powder
- 1/2 teaspoon [3 grams] cream of tartar
- Yellow gel food colorant

Instructions

Preheat oven to 300 Fahrenheit/150 Celsius.

Sift the almond flour and confectioners' sugar together into a bowl. Stir in the arrowroot powder and set aside.

Put a template on a baking sheet and place a silicone mat or parchment

paper over it. Set aside.

In the bowl of a stand mixer, add egg whites and confectioners' sugar. Whisk until well combined.

Place bowl over pot with just enough water, as you don't want the water touching the bowl. Heat on medium until meringue is hot. Test to make sure it's hot enough by sticking your clean finger in the meringue near the center of the bowl. If using a candy thermometer the temperature should be about 130 F [54 C].

Remove from heat and place bowl onto stand mixer. Add the cream of tartar.

Whisk on medium to high speed until firm peaks form. Egg whites should be glossy and if you flip the bowl upside down, nothing will come out.

Add food coloring and whisk until the color is incorporated.

Remove the whisk and add the paddle attachment [if using one].

Add the presifted almond flour and confectioners' sugar mixture.

Turn mixer on low or medium speed and mix for up to 10 seconds. If that doesn't mix the batter thoroughly, mix for another 10 seconds. Turn off mixer and with your spatula, run it around the sides and bottom of bowl to make sure all the dry ingredients are incorporated.

Test for the ribbon stage. When you lift your spatula above the bowl, the batter should fall back to the bowl as one continuous stream and create a ribbon pattern.

Pour batter into a pastry bag [14" or 16"] fitted with a large round tip.

Pipe onto the silicone or parchment covered baking sheets.

When finished with each sheet, bang baking sheet on counter to remove air bubbles. If you see any air bubbles, pop them with a toothpick.

Sprinkle on the chia seeds.

Let shells rest on a flat surface in a cool, dry area for about 30 minutes. The surface will change from glossy to matte. To make sure they're done, gently touch the edge of one with your finger. There should be no trace of batter on your finger.

Bake for 15-20 minutes. This will vary depending on your oven. Carefully monitor the baking process and check your oven thermometer. After 8 or so minutes, rotate the tray to ensure even baking.

Macarons are done when you peel back the mat or the parchment paper and the shells don't stick.

Remove from oven and gently slide the parchment or silicone mat onto a cooling rack. The shells should be cool enough to remove after 10 minutes.

Place macaron shells on a wax paper covered baking sheet or tray for filling. Match similar sized shells together. Pipe the filling on the flat side of one shell and gently place the second shell on top.

White Chocolate Lemon Ganache

Ingredients
- 100 grams [4 ounces] white chocolate chopped
- 50 ml [2 ounces] heavy [double] cream
- Juice of 1 lemon
- Zest of 1 lemon

Instructions
Place the chopped chocolate and cream in a heatproof bowl over a pan of gently simmering water. Don't let the bowl touch the water. Stir occasionally until the chocolate has melted.

Remove from the heat and gradually stir in the lemon juice. Add the zest and mix well. Cover with cling wrap and place the ganache in the fridge until it has become thick, which should take about 2 hours. Or let it sit in a cool dry location overnight.

When the ganache is ready, pipe it onto the macaron shells.

Lingonberry Macarons

Lingonberries are tart like cranberries. They make a lovely contrast to sweet macaron shells.

Ingredients
- 160 grams powdered sugar, sift with almond flour
- 160 grams almond flour, sift with powdered sugar
- 150 grams egg whites
- 180 grams confectioners' sugar, sieved
- 1Tablespoon [8 grams] arrowroot powder
- 1/2 teaspoon [3 grams] cream of tartar
- Purple or pink food gel color

Instructions
Preheat oven to 300 Fahrenheit/150 Celsius.

Sift the almond flour and confectioners' sugar together into a bowl. Stir in the arrowroot powder and set aside.

Put a template on a baking sheet and place a silicone mat or parchment paper over it. Set aside.

In the bowl of a stand mixer, add egg whites and confectioners' sugar.

Whisk until well combined.

Place bowl over steaming pot with just enough water, as you don't want the water touching the bowl. Heat on medium heat until it steams. Test to make sure it's hot enough by sticking your clean finger in the meringue near the center of the bowl. If using a candy thermometer the temperature should be about 130 F [54 C].

Remove from heat and place bowl back onto stand mixer. Add the cream of tartar.

Whisk on medium to high speed until firm peaks form. Egg whites should be glossy and if you flip the bowl upside down, nothing will come out.

Add food coloring and whisk until the color is incorporated.

Remove the whisk and add the paddle attachment [if using one].

Add the presifted almond flour and confectioners' sugar mixture.

Turn mixer to low or medium speed and mix for up to 10 seconds. If that doesn't mix the batter thoroughly, mix for another 10 seconds. Turn off mixer and with your spatula, run it around the sides and bottom of bowl to make sure all the dry ingredients are incorporated.

Test for the ribbon stage. When you lift your spatula above the bowl, the batter should fall back to the bowl as one continuous stream and create a ribbon pattern.

Pour batter into a large pastry bag fitted with a large round tip.

Pipe onto the silicone or parchment covered baking sheets.

When finished with each sheet, bang baking sheet on counter to remove air bubbles. If you see any air bubbles, pop them with a toothpick.

Let shells rest on a flat surface in a cool, dry area for about 30 minutes. The surface will change from glossy to matte. To make sure they're done, gently touch the edge of one with your finger. There should be no trace of batter on your finger.

Bake for 15-20 minutes. This will vary depending on your oven. Carefully monitor the baking process and check your oven thermometer. After 8 or so minutes, rotate the tray to ensure even baking.

Macarons are done when you peel back the mat or the parchment paper and the shells don't stick.

Remove from oven and gently slide the parchment or silicone mat onto a cooling rack. The shells should be cool enough to remove after 10 minutes.

Place macaron shells on a wax paper covered baking sheet or tray for filling. Match similar sized shells together. Pipe the filling on the flat side of one shell and gently place the second shell on top.

Lingonberry Buttercream Filling

Ingredients
- 115 grams [1/2 cup] unsalted butter, room temperature
- 60 ml [1/4 cup] lingonberry jam, strained
- 220 grams [2 cups] confectioners' sugar, sifted
- 1 teaspoon vanilla
- Burgundy gel food colorant

Instructions
Add the butter to the bowl of a stand mixer and mix until creamy. Add the strained lingonberry jam, followed by the confectioners' sugar. Mix on high speed for several minutes. Spoon into a piping bag with a round or star-shaped tip.

Mango Peach Macarons

This is the first batch of macarons I made using the Swiss method.

Ingredients

- 160 grams powdered sugar, sift with almond flour
- 160 grams almond flour, sift with powdered sugar
- 150 grams egg whites
- 180 grams confectioners' sugar, sieved
- 1 Tablespoon [8 grams] arrowroot powder
- 1/2 teaspoon [3 grams] cream of tartar
- Gold food gel colorant

Instructions

Preheat oven to 300 Fahrenheit/150 Celsius.

Sift the almond flour and confectioners' sugar together into a bowl. Stir in the arrowroot powder and set aside.

Put a template on a baking sheet and place a silicone mat or parchment paper over it. Set aside.

In the bowl of a stand mixer, add egg whites and confectioners' sugar. Whisk until well combined.

Place bowl over pot with just enough water, as you don't want the water touching the bowl. Heat on medium until meringue is hot. Test to make sure it's hot enough by sticking your clean finger in the meringue near the center of the bowl. If using a candy thermometer the temperature should be about 130 F [54 C].

Remove from heat and place bowl onto stand mixer. Add the cream of tartar.

Whisk on medium to high speed until firm peaks form. Egg whites should be glossy and if you flip the bowl upside down, nothing will come out.

Add food coloring and whisk until the color is incorporated.

Remove the whisk and add the paddle attachment [if using one].

Add the presifted almond flour and confectioners' sugar mixture.

Turn mixer on low or medium speed and mix for up to 10 seconds. If that doesn't mix the batter thoroughly, mix for another 10 seconds. Turn off mixer and with your spatula, run it around the sides and bottom of bowl to make sure all the dry ingredients are incorporated.

Test for the ribbon stage. When you lift your spatula above the bowl, the batter should fall back to the bowl as one continuous stream and create a ribbon pattern.

Pour batter into a pastry bag [14" or 16"] fitted with a large round tip.

Pipe onto the silicone or parchment covered baking sheets.

When finished with each sheet, bang baking sheet on counter to remove air bubbles. If you see any air bubbles, pop them with a toothpick.

Let shells rest on a flat surface in a cool, dry area for about 30 minutes. The surface will change from glossy to matte. To make sure they're done, gently touch the edge of one with your finger. There should be no trace of batter on your finger.

Bake for 15-20 minutes. This will vary depending on your oven. Carefully monitor the baking process and check your oven thermometer. After 8 or so minutes, rotate the tray to ensure even baking.

Macarons are done when you peel back the mat or the parchment paper and the shells don't stick.

Remove from oven and gently slide the parchment or silicone mat onto a cooling rack. The shells should be cool enough to remove after 10 minutes.

Place macaron shells on a wax paper covered baking sheet or tray for filling. Match similar sized shells together. Pipe the filling on the flat side of one shell and gently place the second shell on top.

Filling – Mango Peach jam – I added an 8-ounce jar to a large piping bag and filled the macarons. You can also use a teaspoon.

Mint Cookies & Cream Macarons

I wanted to make the popular flavor of cookies and cream macarons. When I got to the cookie aisle of the supermarket and saw the mint version, I changed my mind. As a fan of mint, I thought it would be even better than "plain" cookies and cream. It definitely was!

Ingredients

- 160 grams powdered sugar, sift with almond flour
- 160 grams almond flour, sift with powdered sugar
- 150 grams egg whites
- 180 grams confectioners' sugar, sieved
- 1 Tablespoon [8 grams] arrowroot powder
- 1/2 teaspoon [3 grams] cream of tartar
- Mint green gel food colorant
- 2-3 Tablespoons finely crushed mint Oreo cookies for sprinkling

Instructions

Preheat oven to 300 Fahrenheit/150 Celsius.

Sift the almond flour and confectioners' sugar together into a bowl. Stir in the arrowroot powder and set aside.

Put a template on a baking sheet and place a silicone mat or parchment paper over it. Set aside.

In the bowl of a stand mixer, add egg whites and confectioners' sugar. Whisk until well combined.

Place bowl over pot with just enough water, as you don't want the water touching the bowl. Heat on medium until meringue is hot. Test to make sure it's hot enough by sticking your clean finger in the meringue near the center of the bowl. If using a candy thermometer the temperature should be about 130 F [54 C].

Remove from heat and place bowl onto stand mixer. Add the cream of tartar.

Whisk on medium to high speed until firm peaks form. Egg whites should be glossy and if you flip the bowl upside down, nothing will come out.

Add food coloring and whisk until the color is incorporated.

Remove the whisk and add the paddle attachment [if using one].

Add the presifted almond flour and confectioners' sugar mixture.

Turn mixer on low or medium speed and mix for up to 10 seconds. If that doesn't mix the batter thoroughly, mix for another 10 seconds. Turn off mixer and with your spatula, run it around the sides and bottom of bowl to make sure all the dry ingredients are incorporated.

Test for the ribbon stage. When you lift your spatula above the bowl, the batter should fall back to the bowl as one continuous stream and create a ribbon pattern.

Pour batter into a pastry bag [14" or 16"] fitted with a large round tip.

Pipe onto the silicone or parchment covered baking sheets.

When finished with each sheet, bang baking sheet on counter to remove air bubbles. If you see any air bubbles, pop them with a toothpick.

Sprinkle powdered mint Oreo cookies over macaron tops.

Let shells rest on a flat surface in a cool, dry area for about 30 minutes. The surface will change from glossy to matte. To make sure they're done, gently touch the edge of one with your finger. There should be no trace of batter on your finger.

Bake for 15-20 minutes. This will vary depending on your oven. Carefully monitor the baking process and check your oven thermometer. After 8 or so minutes, rotate the tray to ensure even baking.

Macarons are done when you peel back the mat or the parchment paper and the shells don't stick.

Remove from oven and gently slide the parchment or silicone mat onto a cooling rack. The shells should be cool enough to remove after 10 minutes.

Place macaron shells on a wax paper covered baking sheet or tray for filling. Match similar sized shells together. Pipe the filling on the flat side of one shell and gently place the second shell on top.

Oreo Mint Filling

Ingredients

- 64 grams [2.2 ounces] unsalted room temperature butter
- 100 grams [3.5 ounces] cream cheese
- 200 grams [2 cups] powdered sugar, sifted
- 18 Mint Oreo cookies, separate filling and shells [finely crush the Oreo shells]
- Green gel food colorant [optional]
- A few drops of mint essential oil OR ¼ teaspoon mint extract.

Instructions

In a stand mixer with a paddle attachment, mix the butter and cream cheese until smooth and creamy.

Add the powdered sugar, starting at low speed and gradually changing to medium speed. When thoroughly mixed add the cookie filling and mix until the filling is smooth and creamy.

Add a few tablespoons' worth of the crushed Oreo mint cookie shells.

If you want a brighter shade of green, add gel color.

Reserve the rest of the mint Oreo shells to roll on the sides of your sandwiched macaron cookies.

Minty Chocolate Macarons

In my other macaron book, I had a recipe for chocolate mint macarons. The difference in this one is the method of making them. Chocolate mint, minty chocolate, whatever you call it, it's always a winner.

Ingredients

- 160 grams powdered sugar, sift with almond flour
- 160 grams almond flour, sift with powdered sugar
- 150 grams egg whites
- 180 grams confectioners' sugar, sieved
- 1 Tablespoon [8 grams] arrowroot powder
- 1/2 teaspoon [3g] cream of tartar
- Green gel food colorant
- Sprinkles for decorating

Instructions

Preheat oven to 300 Fahrenheit/150 Celsius.

Sift the almond flour and confectioners' sugar together into a bowl. Stir in the arrowroot powder and set aside.

Put a template on a baking sheet and place a silicone mat or parchment

paper over it. Set aside.

In the bowl of a stand mixer, add egg whites and confectioners' sugar. Whisk until well combined.

Place bowl over steaming pot with just enough water, as you don't want the water touching the bowl. Heat on medium heat until it steams. Test to make sure it's hot enough by sticking your clean finger in the meringue near the center of the bowl. If using a candy thermometer the temperature should be about 130 F [54 C].

Remove from heat and place bowl back onto stand mixer. Add the cream of tartar.

Whisk on medium to high speed until firm peaks form. Egg whites should be glossy and if you flip the bowl upside down, nothing will come out.

Add food coloring and whisk until the color is incorporated.

Remove the whisk and add the paddle attachment [if using one].

Add the presifted almond flour and confectioners' sugar mixture.

Turn mixer to low or medium speed and mix for up to 10 seconds. If that doesn't mix the batter thoroughly, mix for another 10 seconds. Turn off mixer and with your spatula, run it around the sides and bottom of bowl to make sure all the dry ingredients are incorporated.

Test for the ribbon stage. When you lift your spatula above the bowl, the batter should fall back to the bowl as one continuous stream and create a ribbon pattern.

Pour batter into a large pastry bag fitted with a large round tip.

Pipe onto the silicone or parchment covered baking sheets.

When finished with each sheet, bang baking sheet on counter to remove air bubbles. If you see any air bubbles, pop them with a toothpick.

Add the sprinkles on top of the macaron shells.

Let shells rest on a flat surface in a cool, dry area for about 30 minutes. The surface will change from glossy to matte. To make sure they're done, gently touch the edge of one with your finger. There should be no trace of batter on your finger.

Bake for 15-20 minutes. This will vary depending on your oven. Carefully monitor the baking process and check your oven thermometer. After 8 or so minutes, rotate the tray to ensure even baking.

Macarons are done when you peel back the mat or the parchment paper and the shells don't stick.

Remove from oven and gently slide the parchment or silicone mat onto a cooling rack. The shells should be cool enough to remove after 10 minutes.

Place macaron shells on a wax paper covered baking sheet or tray for filling. Match similar sized shells together. Pipe the filling on the flat side of one shell and gently place the second shell on top.

Chocolate Mint Ganache Filling

Ingredients
- 120 grams [4 ounces] finely chopped dark chocolate with mint flavor
- 118 ml [4 ounces] heavy [double] cream
- 1 teaspoon vanilla bean paste
- A few drops of mint essential oil OR 1/4 teaspoon mint extract

Instructions
Chop up the mint chocolate and place in a medium glass bowl. Put heavy cream in a small glass container and set microwave timer for 50 seconds. It should be on the verge of boiling. Pour hot cream over chocolate chunks that are in a glass bowl. Whisk both ingredients

together a few times. Add the vanilla bean paste and peppermint. Cover with cling wrap and let sit overnight. The next day, mix once more and spoon into a piping bag.

Pina Colada Macarons

A classic pairing of pineapple and coconut – who can resist the taste of this tempting tropical flavored treat? The buttercream also contains virgin coconut oil and coconut flour for a healthier and nuttier filling!

Ingredients

- 160 g powdered sugar, sift with almond flour
- 160 g almond flour, sift with powdered sugar
- 150 g egg whites
- 180 g confectioners' sugar, sieved
- 1 Tablespoon arrowroot powder
- 1/2 teaspoon [3g] cream of tartar
- Electric yellow food gel
- Shredded coconut or coconut flakes [optional]

Instructions

Preheat oven to 300 Fahrenheit/150 Celsius.

Sift the almond flour and confectioners' sugar together into a bowl. Stir in the arrowroot powder and set aside.

Put a template on a baking sheet and place a silicone mat or parchment

paper over it. Set aside.

In the bowl of a stand mixer, add egg whites and confectioners' sugar. Whisk until well combined.

Place bowl over steaming pot with just enough water, as you don't want the water touching the bowl. Heat on medium heat until it steams. Test to make sure it's hot enough by sticking your clean finger in the meringue near the center of the bowl. If using a candy thermometer the temperature should be about 130 F [54 C].

Remove from heat and place bowl back onto stand mixer. Add the cream of tartar.

Whisk on medium to high speed until firm peaks form. Egg whites should be glossy and if you flip the bowl upside down, nothing will come out.

Add food coloring and whisk until the color is incorporated.

Remove the whisk and add the paddle attachment [if using one].

Add the presifted almond flour and confectioners' sugar mixture.

Turn mixer to low or medium speed and mix for up to 10 seconds. If that doesn't mix the batter thoroughly, mix for another 10 seconds. Turn off mixer and with your spatula, run it around the sides and bottom of bowl to make sure all the dry ingredients are incorporated.

Test for the ribbon stage. When you lift your spatula above the bowl, the batter should fall back to the bowl as one continuous stream and create a ribbon pattern.

Pour batter into a large pastry bag fitted with a large round tip.

Pipe onto the silicone or parchment covered baking sheets.

Sprinkle shredded coconut or coconut flakes on tops of shells [optional].

When finished with each sheet, bang baking sheet on counter to

remove air bubbles. If you see any air bubbles, pop them with a toothpick.

Let shells rest on a flat surface in a cool, dry area for about 30 minutes. The surface will change from glossy to matte. To make sure they're done, gently touch the edge of one with your finger. There should be no trace of batter on your finger.

Bake for 15-20 minutes. This will vary depending on your oven. Carefully monitor the baking process and check your oven thermometer. After 8 or so minutes, rotate the tray to ensure even baking.

Macarons are done when you peel back the mat or the parchment paper and the shells don't stick.

Remove from oven and gently slide the parchment or silicone mat onto a cooling rack. The shells should be cool enough to remove after 10 minutes.

Place macaron shells on a wax paper covered baking sheet or tray for filling. Match similar sized shells together. Pipe the filling on the flat side of one shell and gently place the second shell on top.

Pineapple & Coconut [Pina Colada] Filling

This is a recipe I made up due to being a coconut lover. I used coconut flour, which is very dry, and it helps the pineapple coconut jam incorporate better since it was a slightly runny jam. If you can't find pineapple coconut jam, simply use pineapple jam, which is much easier to find.

Ingredients
- 125 grams [4 ounces] unsalted butter, room temperature
- 2 ounces virgin coconut oil, solid
- 3 Tablespoons coconut flour
- 125 grams [1 cup] confectioners' sugar, sifted

- 60 grams [1/4 cup] pineapple & coconut jam
- 1 teaspoon vanilla
- 3 drops lemon yellow food color gel

Instructions

In the bowl of a stand mixer, mix butter and virgin coconut oil together for a few minutes. When well incorporated, add the coconut flour, pineapple and coconut jam, and confectioners' sugar. Mix for about 5-7 minutes and add the colorant. Spoon into a piping bag.

Variations: sprinkle shredded or flaked coconut on the top of the macaron shells.

Add a few tablespoons of shredded or flaked coconut on a plate so you can roll on the sides of your sandwiched macaron cookies.

Raspberry Cheesecake Macarons

How easy is it to make a delicious cheesecake frosting? I was surprised at how simple it was. And you can make it in any of your favorite flavors.

Ingredients

- 160 grams powdered sugar, sift with almond flour
- 160 grams almond flour, sift with powdered sugar
- 150 grams egg whites
- 180 grams confectioners' sugar, sieved
- 1 Tablespoon [8 grams] arrowroot powder
- 1/2 teaspoon [3 grams] cream of tartar
- Pink gel food colorant

Instructions

Preheat oven to 300 Fahrenheit/150 Celsius.

Sift the almond flour and confectioners' sugar together into a bowl. Stir in the arrowroot powder and set aside.

Put a template on a baking sheet and place a silicone mat or parchment paper over it. Set aside.

In the bowl of a stand mixer, add egg whites and confectioners' sugar. Whisk until well combined.

Place bowl over pot with just enough water, as you don't want the water touching the bowl. Heat on medium until meringue is hot. Test to make sure it's hot enough by sticking your clean finger in the meringue near the center of the bowl. If using a candy thermometer the temperature should be about 130 F [54 C].

Remove from heat and place bowl onto stand mixer. Add the cream of tartar.

Whisk on medium to high speed until firm peaks form. Egg whites should be glossy and if you flip the bowl upside down, nothing will come out.

Add food coloring and whisk until the color is incorporated.

Remove the whisk and add the paddle attachment [if using one].

Add the presifted almond flour and confectioners' sugar mixture.

Turn mixer on low or medium speed and mix for up to 10 seconds. If that doesn't mix the batter thoroughly, mix for another 10 seconds. Turn off mixer and with your spatula, run it around the sides and bottom of bowl to make sure all the dry ingredients are incorporated.

Test for the ribbon stage. When you lift your spatula above the bowl, the batter should fall back to the bowl as one continuous stream and create a ribbon pattern.

Pour batter into a pastry bag [14" or 16"] fitted with a large round tip.

Pipe onto the silicone or parchment covered baking sheets.

When finished with each sheet, bang baking sheet on counter to remove air bubbles. If you see any air bubbles, pop them with a toothpick.

Let shells rest on a flat surface in a cool, dry area for about 30 minutes.

The surface will change from glossy to matte. To make sure they're done, gently touch the edge of one with your finger. There should be no trace of batter on your finger.

Bake for 15-20 minutes. This will vary depending on your oven. Carefully monitor the baking process and check your oven thermometer. After 8 or so minutes, rotate the tray to ensure even baking.

Macarons are done when you peel back the mat or the parchment paper and the shells don't stick.

Remove from oven and gently slide the parchment or silicone mat onto a cooling rack. The shells should be cool enough to remove after 10 minutes.

Place macaron shells on a wax paper covered baking sheet or tray for filling. Match similar sized shells together. Pipe the filling on the flat side of one shell and gently place the second shell on top.

Raspberry Cheesecake Filling

Ingredients
- 170 grams [6 ounces] cream cheese, softened
- 110 grams [1/3 cup] raspberry jam
- 1 teaspoon vanilla bean paste
- 313 grams [2 1/2 cups] confectioner's sugar, sifted
- Red and pink gel food colorants for striping bag

Instructions
Place the softened cream cheese into a mixing bowl and beat on high speed for several minutes until creamy. Add the raspberry jam, and vanilla. Mix again until creamy. Add confectioner's sugar, mixing well until the frosting thickens.

Using a clean paintbrush, paint stripes into a large pastry bag. Insert into a tall glass or jug so it's easier to spoon the filling into the bag.

Strawberry Rhubarb Macarons

The perfect sweet and tart combination of fruits is what makes these macarons so delicious.

Ingredients
- 160 grams powdered sugar, sift with almond flour
- 160 grams almond flour, sift with powdered sugar
- 150 grams egg whites
- 180 grams confectioners' sugar, sieved
- 1Tablespoon arrowroot powder
- 1/2 teaspoon [3g] cream of tartar
- 2 teaspoons vanilla bean paste
- Red or dark pink food color gel

Instructions
Preheat oven to 300 Fahrenheit/150 Celsius.

Sift the almond flour and confectioners' sugar together into a bowl. Stir in the arrowroot powder and set aside.

Put a template on a baking sheet and place a silicone mat or parchment paper over it. Set aside.

In the bowl of a stand mixer, add egg whites and confectioners' sugar. Whisk until well combined.

Place bowl over steaming pot with just enough water, as you don't want the water touching the bowl. Heat on medium heat until it steams. Test to make sure it's hot enough by sticking your clean finger in the meringue near the center of the bowl. If using a candy thermometer the temperature should be about 130 F [54 C].

Remove from heat and place bowl back onto stand mixer. Add the cream of tartar.

Whisk on medium to high speed until firm peaks form. Egg whites should be glossy and if you flip the bowl upside down, nothing will come out.

Add vanilla bean paste and food coloring and whisk until the color is incorporated.

Remove the whisk and add the paddle attachment [if using one].

Add the presifted almond flour and confectioners' sugar mixture.

Turn mixer to low or medium speed and mix for up to 10 seconds. If that doesn't mix the batter thoroughly, mix for another 10 seconds. Turn off mixer and with your spatula, run it around the sides and bottom of bowl to make sure all the dry ingredients are incorporated.

Test for the ribbon stage. When you lift your spatula above the bowl, the batter should fall back to the bowl as one continuous stream and create a ribbon pattern.

Pour batter into a large pastry bag fitted with a large round tip.

Pipe onto the silicone or parchment covered baking sheets.

When finished with each sheet, bang baking sheet on counter to remove air bubbles. If you see any air bubbles, pop them with a toothpick.

Let shells rest on a flat surface in a cool, dry area for about 30 minutes.

The surface will change from glossy to matte. To make sure they're done, gently touch the edge of one with your finger. There should be no trace of batter on your finger.

Bake for 15-20 minutes. This will vary depending on your oven. Carefully monitor the baking process and check your oven thermometer. After 8 or so minutes, rotate the tray to ensure even baking.

Macarons are done when you peel back the mat or the parchment paper and the shells don't stick.

Remove from oven and gently slide the parchment or silicone mat onto a cooling rack. The shells should be cool enough to remove after 10 minutes.

Place macaron shells on a wax paper covered baking sheet or tray for filling. Match similar sized shells together. Pipe the filling on the flat side of one shell and gently place the second shell on top.

Strawberry Rhubarb Mascarpone Filling

Ingredients
- 125 grams [4 ounces] mascarpone, room temperature
- 125 grams [4 ounces] unsalted butter, room temperature
- 40 grams [heaping 1/3 cup] confectioners' sugar, sifted
- 60 grams [1/4 cup] strawberry rhubarb jam
- 1 Tablespoon honey
- 2 teaspoons vanilla bean paste
- Red or dark pink food color gel

Instructions
In the bowl of a stand mixer, mix mascarpone and butter together for a few minutes. When well incorporated, add the vanilla, strawberry rhubarb jam, and confectioners' sugar. Mix for a few minutes and add the colorant. Spoon into a piping bag. For a decorative touch, use a star piping tip.

Zesty Lime Macarons

As a huge fan of citrus fruits, I'd made lime macarons before. This was the first time I made a lime ganache and it's as wonderful as the lemon ganache.

Ingredients

- 160 grams powdered sugar, sift with almond flour
- 160 grams almond flour, sift with powdered sugar
- 150 grams egg whites
- 180 grams confectioners' sugar, sieved
- 1 Tablespoon lime zest
- 1 Tablespoon [8 grams] arrowroot powder
- 1/2 teaspoon [3 grams] cream of tartar
- Green food gel colorant

Instructions

Preheat oven to 300 Fahrenheit/150 Celsius.

Sift the almond flour and confectioners' sugar together into a bowl. Stir in the arrowroot powder and set aside.

Put a template on a baking sheet and place a silicone mat or parchment

paper over it. Set aside.

In the bowl of a stand mixer, add egg whites and confectioners' sugar. Whisk until well combined.

Place bowl over pot with just enough water, as you don't want the water touching the bowl. Heat on medium until meringue is hot. Test to make sure it's hot enough by sticking your clean finger in the meringue near the center of the bowl. If using a candy thermometer the temperature should be about 130 F [54 C].

Remove from heat and place bowl onto stand mixer. Add the cream of tartar.

Whisk on medium to high speed until firm peaks form. Egg whites should be glossy and if you flip the bowl upside down, nothing will come out.

Add food coloring and whisk until the color is incorporated.

Remove the whisk and add the paddle attachment [if using one].

Add the presifted almond flour and confectioners' sugar mixture.

Turn mixer on low or medium speed and mix for up to 10 seconds. If that doesn't mix the batter thoroughly, mix for another 10 seconds. Turn off mixer and with your spatula, run it around the sides and bottom of bowl to make sure all the dry ingredients are incorporated.

Test for the ribbon stage. When you lift your spatula above the bowl, the batter should fall back to the bowl as one continuous stream and create a ribbon pattern.

Pour batter into a pastry bag [14" or 16"] fitted with a large round tip.

Pipe onto the silicone or parchment covered baking sheets.

When finished with each sheet, bang baking sheet on counter to remove air bubbles. If you see any air bubbles, pop them with a toothpick.

Sprinkle lime zest over the macarons.

Let shells rest on a flat surface in a cool, dry area for about 30 minutes. The surface will change from glossy to matte. To make sure they're done, gently touch the edge of one with your finger. There should be no trace of batter on your finger.

Bake for 15-20 minutes. This will vary depending on your oven. Carefully monitor the baking process and check your oven thermometer. After 8 or so minutes, rotate the tray to ensure even baking.

Macarons are done when you peel back the mat or the parchment paper and the shells don't stick.

Remove from oven and gently slide the parchment or silicone mat onto a cooling rack. The shells should be cool enough to remove after 10 minutes.

Place macaron shells on a wax paper covered baking sheet or tray for filling. Match similar sized shells together. Pipe the filling on the flat side of one shell and gently place the second shell on top.

White Chocolate Lime Ganache

Ingredients
- 100 grams [4 ounces] white chocolate, chopped
- 60 ml [1/4 cup] heavy [double] cream
- Juice of 1 lime
- Zest of 1 lime

Instructions
Place the chopped chocolate and cream in a heatproof bowl over a pan of gently simmering water. Don't let the bowl touch the water. Stir occasionally until the chocolate has melted.

Remove from the heat and gradually stir in the lime juice. Add the zest and mix well. Cover with cling wrap and place the ganache in the fridge until it has become thick, which should take about 2 hours. Or let it sit in a cool dry location overnight.

When the ganache is ready, pipe it onto the macaron shells.

CHAPTER 10
THE RECIPE GUIDE

The following recipe guide may seem excessively detailed or maybe it's not detailed enough; that's for you to decide. Initially, I didn't intend to take extensive notes as I only planned to make one batch of macarons. Then I decided to try another batch, and another. Each time, I'd write notes and it just grew into a habit.

By the way, before I ever referred to each recipe as a batch, I used the word attempt. After a dozen tries, I decided I was doing more than attempting to bake macarons--they really were batches!

Before you begin, please do an ingredients checklist. Make certain you have all the ingredients and necessary equipment. Also, make sure your mixing bowls are super clean, as are your silicone mats, if using them. A few times, I've found stray cat hairs in the bowls and on the mats, so I've learned to carefully check them.

- Date and time.
- Temperature and humidity.
- Name/flavor of macaron recipe.
- Batch number [optional].
- Sift/process almond flour.
- Sift confectioners' sugar.
- Add arrowroot powder.
- Separate eggs.
- Premix confectioners' sugar and egg whites.
- Cook sugar/egg whites to 125-130 Fahrenheit/50-55 Celsius.
- Start meringue.
- Add cream of tartar.
- Time when meringue has reached firm peak.

- Note if you're adding color and what type [gel, liquid or powder].
- Number of seconds mixing batter in mixer [mixer macaronage].
- Finish macaronage by hand, so you don't miss any unmixed areas at the bottom or the top of the whisk/paddle attachment.
- When piping: note the time you started piping each tray.
- Count the number of shells on each tray.
- Set oven temperature [if you haven't already done so].
- If you haven't already made the filling previously, make your filling.
- Once your macarons have rested for at least 30 minutes, make sure they're done and add the first baking sheet.
- Note the oven temperature and the time.
- Halfway through baking, rotate the tray. Check the oven temperature to see if it's changed.
- When the shells are done, put on cooling rack and rest for about 10 minutes.
- Check oven temperature before adding the second tray.
- Remove macaron shells from first tray and place on waxed paper covered flat surface.
- When all the macaron shells are finished, fill them.
- Store and label your macarons in an airtight container. If you refrigerate them, they'll be ready to eat within 12-24 hours. If you freeze them, they'll last for about 3 months. If freezing, label and date them.
- If you have extra filling, it can be saved in the refrigerator for about a week, and in the freezer for about a month. Label and date your filling.

CHAPTER 11
RESOURCES

Where do you get your ingredients and supplies? That answer will mostly like be your supermarket, crafts store, discount, kitchen store, department store or online specialty shop.

Almond Flour
- King Arthur
  http://www.kingarthurflour.com/shop/items/almond-flour-1-lb
- Bob's Red Mill super-fine almond flour from blanched whole almonds
  http://www.bobsredmill.com/almond-meal-flour.html
- Mandelin ~ Growers and handlers of superb quality almonds and manufacturers of premium almond pastes and almond products.
  https://www.mandelininc.com/shop/blanched-almond-flour/

Sugar, Confectioners' / Icing
- East Coast
  https://www.dominosugar.com/sugar/confectioners-sugar
- West Coast
  https://www.chsugar.com/products/confectioners-sugar

Cocoa Powder
- Trader Joe's Cocoa Powder [not listed on website but they carry it in their stores].
- Valrhona
  https://www.valrhona-chocolate.com

Chocolate Bars
- Green & Black's https://www.greenandblacks.co.uk
- Valrhona https://www.valrhona-chocolate.com
- Amazon https://www.amazon.com

Butterscotch
- Guittard https://www.guittard.com/our-chocolate/detail/butterscotch-baking-chips

Colors
- AmeriColor https://www.americolorcorp.com/
- Gel pastes, airbrush and powdered colors. Chefmaster. https://chefmaster.la/collections/liqua-gel
- Liqua-gel food colors and natural plant-based liqua-gel food colors.
- Colorants Confection Crafts colorant http://confectioncrafts.com/shop/natural-colors/natural-powder-colors.html
- Lorann Food coloring powder http://www.lorannoils.com/powder-food-coloring
- Wilton http://www.wilton.com/icing-color/pg_icingColors.html
- Wilton neon gel food colors https://www.amazon.com/Wilton-Neon-Gel-Food-Color/dp/B007EMYD8M
- Gourmet Writer Food Decorator Pens AmeriColor https://www.americolorcorp.com/product/10-color-gourmet-writer-sets/

Bakeware
- Cookie sheets

- Nordic Ware Baker's Half Sheet
- Nordic Ware
  https://www.nordicware.com/catalog/product/view/id/2242/s/baker-s-half-sheet/category/48/
- Wilton
  http://www.wilton.com/17x11-jelly-roll-pan/2105-968.html#start=6
- NOTE: Whether a jelly roll pan or a cookie sheet is used, please remember to cover it with a silicone mat OR parchment paper!

Parchment Paper

- Reynolds
  http://www.reynoldskitchens.com/parchment-paper/parchment-paper-rolls/ [rolls]
  http://www.reynoldskitchens.com/parchment-paper/ [sheets]
- Natural unbleached parchment paper
  https://www.kingarthurflour.com/shop/items/natural-parchment-paper-set-of-50

Silicone Mats

- Amazon Basics
  https://www.amazon.com/AmazonBasics-Silicone-Baking-Mat-Pack/dp/B00V5IM0EU
- Silpat
  http://silpat.com/products.html
- Amazon
  https://www.amazon.com/Silpat-AE420295-07-Premium-Non-Stick-Silicone/dp/B00008T960/
- Velesco
  https://velescoinc.com/product/silicone-baking-mats/
- Amazon
  https://www.amazon.com/Silicone-Baking-Mat-Professional-Nonstick/dp/B00Y5VO6HS

- Simple Baker Premium Silicone Baking Mat for Macarons
  https://www.amazon.com/Simple-Baker-Premium-Silicone-Macarons/dp/B015MMI9EE

Digital Scales
- Amazon
  https://www.amazon.com/Digital-Kitchen-Scales/b?ie=UTF8&node=678508011
- Bed Bath & Beyond
  https://www.bedbathandbeyond.com/store/s/kitchen-digital-scale?ta=typeahead

Vanilla Bean Paste
- Nielsen Massey
  https://nielsenmassey.com/products/pure-vanilla-bean-paste
- Cook's
  https://www.cooksvanilla.com/product/pure-vanilla-bean-puree-paste/

Almond & Other Extracts
- Cook's
  https://www.cooksvanilla.com/product/organic-pure-almond-extract/
- McCormick
  https://www.mccormick.com/spices-and-flavors/extracts-and-food-colors/extracts

Piping Bags & Tips
- Ateco carries piping bags and tips [decorating tubes]
  http://www.atecousa.com/decorating-bags.html
- Piping tips/decorating tubes
  http://www.atecousa.com/all-decorating-tubes-3.html
  [Recommend sizes: 802-806]
- Kootek piping bags – 16-inch
  https://www.ikootek.com/kitchen

- Amazon

  https://www.amazon.com/dp/B06XT16237

  https://www.amazon.com/Wilton-Disposable-16-Inch-Decorating-Bags/dp/B00175TFJ4/

  https://www.amazon.com/dp/B00FGVD8UW/ref=psdc_13825881_t1_B0043UJERS

- Wilton disposable 16-inch bags

  http://www.wilton.com/16-inch-disposable-piping-bags/2104-1357.html#q=16%22+piping+bags&start=13

- Wilton tips – this is a 4-pack of large tips which includes 2 round and 2 star tips. This was the original set I bought to get started.

  http://www.wilton.com/large-icing-tip-set/418-6608.html#start=5

Other stores with baking supplies:

- Bed Bath & Beyond https://www.bedbathandbeyond.com
- Hobby Lobby http://www.hobbylobby.com
- Jo-Ann Fabric and Crafts Stores http://www.joann.com
- Michaels Arts & Crafts http://www.michaels.com
- Sur la Table http://www.surlatable.com
- Williams-Sonoma http://www.williams-sonoma.com

CHAPTER 12
RECOMMENDED BOOKS & WEBSITES

Books:

Les Petits Macarons:
Colorful French Confections to Make at Home by Kathryn Gordon & Anne E. McBride [this book has photos and a recipe for the Swiss meringue method].

https://www.amazon.com/Petits-Macarons-Colorful-French-Confections-ebook/dp/B005QBKXQO

Sweet Macarons: Delectable French Confections for Every Day by Mercotte
This book mentions the Swiss method but also includes directions for mixing French and Italian meringue macaron batter in a stand mixer.

https://www.amazon.com/Sweet-Macarons-Delectable-French-Confections/dp/1600854990

Websites:

Facebook Group – Macarons, Tips, Techniques & Tricks
A place where those who are interested in learning how to make macarons, can share, get tips, recipes, share their cookies and make new friends.

https://www.facebook.com/groups/allthingsmacs

Article entitled "Of ovens and baking [and macarons]"
http://www.syrupandtang.com/201003/of-ovens-and-baking-and-macarons/

Temperature Conversion Calculator
http://www.traditionaloven.com/conversions_of_measures/temperature

_units.html

Conversion of Measurements
http://www.convertunits.com/from/grams/to/cups

Macaron Templates
I recommend the second to the last one entitled "Macaron Template PDF" or the last one entitled "Free Macaron Template."

https://www.sampletemplates.com/business-templates/macaron-template.html

Watch for more macaron baking tutorials on my YouTube channel:
https://www.youtube.com/user/LisaMaliga

Please click to subscribe.

ABOUT THE AUTHOR

Thank you for taking the time to read *Baking Macarons: The Swiss Meringue Method*. Feel free to leave a review at your favorite online bookstore. Also, tell your friends, family and local library about this book, along with any of my other titles!

Happy Baking!

Lisa Maliga is an American author of contemporary fiction, psychological thrillers and cozy mysteries. Her nonfiction titles consist of how to make bath and body products with an emphasis on melt and pour soap crafting. When researching her cozy mystery, she discovered the art of baking French macarons. She continues to bake macarons, always trying new flavor combinations. When not writing, Lisa reads an assortment of books, takes photos, and is working on a series of baking and soaping video tutorials.

You'll find more about her work at:

- http://www.lisamaliga.com
- http://lisamaliga.wordpress.com
- http://pinterest.com/lisamaliga
- https://twitter.com/LisaMaliga
- http://www.goodreads.com/LisaMaliga
- https://www.youtube.com/user/LisaMaliga Soapcrafting & baking tutorials
- http://eepurl.com/UZbE9 The Discerning Readers' Newsletter ~ Sign up to receive news of forthcoming books, free eBooks, gift cards & more!

Made in the USA
Middletown, DE
23 October 2023

41277576R10086